Martin Booth

111
in I
Tha. You
Shouldn't Miss

D0628463

Photographs by Barbara Evripidou

(111)

emons:

For Mersina and Lois
Martin Booth

For my Mum & Dad
Barbara Evripidou

© Emons Verlag GmbH
All rights reserved
© Photographs by Barbara Evripidou, except:
Paul Blakemore (p. 240, top), Michael Lloyd (p. 240, bottom)
© Cover icon: shutterstock.com/Southtownboy Studio
Layout: Eva Kraskes, based on a design by Lübbeke | Naumann | Thoben
Maps: altancicek.design, www.altancicek.de
Basic cartographical information from Openstreetmap,
© OpenStreetMap-Mitwirkende, OdbL
Editing: Alison Lester
Printing and binding: Grafisches Centrum Cuno, Calbe
Printed in Germany 2020
ISBN 978-3-7408-0898-3
First edition

Did you enjoy this guidebook? Would you like to see more?
Join us in uncovering new places around the world on:
www.111places.com

Foreword

Bristol made international headlines as we were putting the finishing touches to this guide. A statue of notorious slave trader, Edward Colston, that had been standing for 125 years, was toppled from its plinth on 7 June, 2020 and unceremoniously dumped into the docks. As a journalist, I was reporting on the Black Lives Matter march that was taking place the same day. On that famous afternoon, I found myself next to the statue lying on the ground as a masked man knelt on its neck for 8 minutes and 46 seconds, a symbolic act in memory of George Floyd who had died only a week earlier in Minnesota after his own neck was knelt on by police.

In the days after the statue was toppled, I watched as the nearby Colston Hall removed its exterior signage ahead of the announcement of a new name, and I reported that schools across the city named after Colston would begin a process of deciding whether to change their own names. As the eyes of the world were on us, I had never felt prouder to call Bristol my home.

I was born in Bristol but moved away when I was very young as my dad's job took the family to Hertfordshire. But I moved back and have now lived here for a dozen years. Every day I still find new reasons to love my city, not least the fact that my two Bristolian daughters allow me to see Bristol once again with new eyes. I regularly cycle home along the Floating Harbour, with the SS *Great Britain* just across the water and the colourful houses of Cliftonwood in the distance. It's a picture-postcard view of a special place that I hope, with the help of this book, you will also fall in love with. Come and visit during St Paul's Carnival, an extraordinary celebration of African and Caribbean culture when the area comes alive with a colourful parade, sound systems on street corners and a world of different flavours. That's Bristol in a nutshell. We dance to our own rhythm.

Martin Booth

111 Places

1 __ 20th Century Flicks
The UK's last video shop and smallest multiplex | 10

2 __ acta Community Theatre
No need to audition | 12

3 __ Alfred Fagon Statue
A trailblazing actor and playwright | 14

4 __ The Architecture Centre
A hub for design and the built environment | 16

5 __ Arnos Vale Cemetery
From garden cemetery to wilderness to restoration | 18

6 __ Averys
Wine from the mists of time | 20

7 __ The Bag of Nails
The cat pub | 22

8 __ The Balmoral
Hoping for new nautical adventures | 24

9 __ Barton Hill Settlement
A vital community resource | 26

10 __ The Bearpit
The travails of a sunken roundabout | 28

11 __ Beese's
Messing about on the river | 30

12 __ The Black Castle
A weird and wonderful folly | 32

13 __ Boiling Wells
The clue is in the name | 34

14 __ Bottle Yard Studios
The Hollywood of the South West | 36

15 __ Brandy Bottom Colliery
A rare example of a largely forgotten industry | 38

16 __ Bristol & Bath Railway Path
A daily pedal rather than a daily grind | 40

17 __ Bristol Bike Project
Love on two wheels | 42

18 __ Bristol Bus Boycott
A watershed moment for UK civil rights | 44

19___ Bristol Castle
Still visible if you look closely | 46

20___ Bristol Cathedral Garden
A small oasis of calm | 48

21___ Bristol Central Library
Books in breathtaking spaces | 50

22___ Bristol County Ground
Reflecting cricket's place in the city | 52

23___ Bristol Improv Theatre
The UK's first venue dedicated to improv | 54

24___ BWRP
Transforming waste into shared assets | 56

25___ Broadmead Baptist Church
The church above the shops | 58

26___ Brunel's Buttery
Banging bacon butties | 60

27___ Brunel's Other Bridge
An abandoned piece of engineering history | 62

28___ Business As Usual
The unofficial home of Bristol cycling | 64

29___ Cafe Wall Illusion
An accidental trick of the eye | 66

30___ Campus Pool Skatepark
Where skating has replaced splashing | 68

31___ Castle Park Pyramid
Going underground | 70

32___ Chance & Counters
Fancy a game? | 72

33___ Charles Wesley's House
A home of hymns | 74

34___ Chatterton's Cafe
Paninis and poetry | 76

35___ Cheers Drive
Bristol's very own Boaty McBoatface | 78

36___ Cider at the Orchard
Enjoy some West Country champagne | 80

37___ Circomedia
Run away to join the circus | 82

38___ Clifton Rocks Railway
A fun and fascinating funicular | 84

MAIN
ENTRANCE

39___ Clifton Rock Slide
Polished smooth by generations of bottoms | 86

40___ Convoy Espresso
Cracking coffee in converted caravans | 88

41___ Cross-harbour Ferry
A fun way to get from A to B | 90

42___ The Cube
Much more than just a cinema | 92

43___ Cumberland Piazza
Under-flyover art | 94

44___ Dowry Square
Find yourself in hot water | 96

45___ Everard's Printing Works
An Art Nouveau advertisement | 98

46___ Elizabeth Blackwell's House
Prejudice-fighting female physician | 100

47___ The Exchange
A music venue owned by music fans | 102

48___ Felix Road Playground
Get the kids outdoors! | 104

49___ Folk House
From working folk to folk music | 106

50___ Friendly Records
A vinyl revival | 108

51___ Glitch
A passion for innovation | 110

52___ Goat Gully
Hairy conservationists | 112

53___ Goldney Hall Grotto
A subterranean treasure | 114

54___ Guilbert's
Home to Bristol's own Oompa Loompas | 116

55___ Hart's Bakery
From bondage to bread | 118

56___ Henleaze Lake
Swim in a former quarry | 120

57___ The High Cross
Can we have it back please? | 122

58___ High Kingsdown
A low-rise architectural marvel | 124

59 ___ Horfield Common Urinal
A Moorish-style men's room | 126

60 ___ Incredible Edible
Growing food on street corners | 128

61 ___ Ken Stradling Collection
One man's passion for beautiful objects | 130

62 ___ Kiln Restaurant
Once the hottest place in town | 132

63 ___ Kings Weston Roman Villa
Marooned Roman remains | 134

64 ___ Knowle West Media Centre
Made of straw, but solid as a rock | 136

65 ___ Letterpress Collective
An ancient trade revived | 138

66 ___ Lollypop-Be-Bop
A little bit of magic | 140

67 ___ Lord Mayor's Chapel
The only church of its kind in the UK | 142

68 ___ Metalgnu
A metal menagerie | 144

69 ___ Milliners' Guild
A hat for every occasion | 146

70 ___ Mina Road Tunnel
An ever-changing street-art canvas | 148

71 ___ Mr Langford's Plaque
Time waits for no man | 150

72 ___ Napier Square
A one-sided square | 152

73 ___ Nicholas Cage Pub Sign
'Put…the bunny…back…in the box' | 154

74 ___ Nipper Statue
Bristol's most famous musical icon? | 156

75 ___ Palestine Museum
The history of Palestine in a former nightclub | 158

76 ___ The Passenger Shed
A cathedral-like former railway station | 160

77 ___ Paul Dirac Memorial
Better at maths than Einstein | 162

78 ___ Pipe Walk
Water everywhere; no longer a drop to drink | 164

79___ Prince Rupert's Gate
A reminder of Bristol's role in the English Civil War | 166

80___ Psychopomp
A distillery disguised as a greengrocer's | 168

81___ Quakers' Burial Ground
A hermit, lead shot and a runaway car | 170

82___ Recession
Retro clothes, records, repartee and more | 172

83___ Redland Standing Stone
A mysterious monolith | 174

84___ River Frome
Bristol's lost river | 176

85___ Room 212
At the heart of Bristol's art scene | 178

86___ Royal Fort Garden
A jewel in the heart of the University | 180

87___ St Bartholomew's Hospital
Ships and skeletons on a Saxon site | 182

88___ St Edith's Well
Only recently rediscovered | 184

89___ St Mary le Port
Fans of abandoned spaces? This one's for you! | 186

90___ St Philip's Footbridge
The £3m bridge to nowhere | 188

91___ St Werburgh's City Farm
Pigs in the city | 190

92___ Sea Mills Museum
A memorable use for an old telephone box | 192

93___ Seven Saints of St Paul's
Honouring seven esteemed legacies | 194

94___ Severn Beach Line
Escape to the country | 196

95___ South Bristol Berry Maze
Forage for free in the city | 198

96___ Stokes Croft China
'Peculiar china for a peculiar society' | 200

97___ Sweetmart
The world's flavours under one roof | 202

98___ Temple Church
Bristol's own leaning tower of Pisa | 204

99 — That Thing
Fabulous festival fashion | 206

100 — Thunder Run
18th-century surround sound | 208

101 — Tobacco Factory Market
A symbol of regeneration | 210

102 — Tramway Rail Monument
A lasting memory of the Bristol Blitz | 212

103 — Trinity
Birthplace of the Bristol Sound | 214

104 — Troopers Hill
Industrial past, wildlife present | 216

105 — Unicorns
Mythical? They're everywhere! | 218

106 — UoB Theatre Collection
Centuries-old treasures still inspiring new work | 220

107 — Vale Street
The steepest residential road in the UK | 222

108 — Wellington T2905 Memorial
Not your usual balloon ride | 224

109 — Westbury College
A castle in miniature | 226

110 — The Wicker Nose
An enormous olfactory edifice | 228

111 — Zion
Deconsecrated, but far from dead | 230

1 20th Century Flicks

The UK's last video shop and smallest multiplex

In its former Clifton premises, 20th Century Flicks counted University of Bristol students such as Simon Pegg among its members. (The Gloucestershire-born actor and comedian allegedly still owes £4.50 for a late VHS copy of *Crimes and Misdemeanours*.) When it opened in Redland in 1982, video stores were still ubiquitous. Today, 20th Century Flicks is unique.

In an age of streaming films at the click of a remote control, there's something comforting about a shop where staff can make recommendations based on a conversation about your preferences rather than an algorithm. Here is an unrivalled collection of more than 20,000 films, patrolled by a cat called Poppy, with new movies costing £4 for three nights' rental, and all others available for £2 for seven nights. The shop had one of the world's first searchable computer databases, which could have been an influence on Col Needham, who founded IMDb from his Bristol bedroom. With legal and illegal downloading causing a dramatic slump in the lucrative student market, coupled with a dramatic rent increase, a successful crowd-funding campaign in 2014 financed a move to these council-owned (and rent-controlled) premises on Christmas Steps, with a few dozen regular customers helping to move the thousands of DVDs and VHS cassettes to their new home.

The traditional video rental shop area is now bookended by the two smallest cinemas in Bristol: the 11-seat Kino and the 18-seat Videodrome, which contains original 1920s' seats from the Bristol Hippodrome. Opening the two mini cinemas was an undoubted risk for co-owners David Taylor and Dave White, but their introduction has seen an upturn in fortunes for 20th Century Flicks, with a new revenue stream and an influx of potential new customers, as there can't be many children in the city who haven't been invited for a birthday-party screening at the world's longest running video shop.

Address 19 Christmas Steps, BS1 5BS, +44(0)117 925 8432, info@20thcenturyflicks.co.uk, www.20thcenturyflicks.co.uk | Getting there 5-minute walk from Bristol bus station | Hours Daily 1–8pm | Tip The current three-screen Orpheus Cinema in Henleaze was built on the site of the original Orpheus, which opened in 1938 with 1,400 seats and was demolished in 1972. Its replacement is now located above a Waitrose supermarket (bristolwestburypark.scottcinemas.co.uk).

2 acta Community Theatre

No need to audition

You don't have to go far in Bristol to find a theatre, or spaces in which theatre is performed. Above a pub is the Alma Tavern Theatre; just 12 people at a time were able to see the first-ever theatre performances staged within the vaults of the Clifton Suspension Bridge; south of the river, the Tobacco Factory Theatres play in a former tobacco factory; and promenade theatre experts Show of Strength have put on shows focusing on the slave trade and some of the area's more unusual characters.

Also south of the river, between North Street and West Street in Bedminster, is one of the UK's leading community theatres, which celebrated its 35th anniversary in September 2020. acta aims to engage people who are not connected to the cultural life of Bristol, including isolated older people; migrants, refugees and asylum seekers; vulnerable young people; disabled people; and people living outside the city centre where most of Bristol's opportunities to access the arts are located. The company are specialists at developing a new audience for theatre with more than a dozen original shows created every year.

'We believe that theatre belongs to everyone, and everyone has a story to tell,' wrote acta co-founder Neil Beddow in a blog post to mark the organisation's 35 years. The acronym came before it was decided what it should stand for, which was eventually chosen to be Avon Community Theatre Agency. The company's early days saw it working in a youth club in Hartcliffe, and setting up youth theatres in areas including Lockleaze and Knowle West, among the most underprivileged corners not only of Bristol but also of the UK.

Today, community members create and perform original drama which is rooted in their own experiences and stories. There is never an audition, as people from some of the city's most deprived areas continue to use theatre to express and overcome their struggles.

Address Gladstone Street, Bedminster, BS3 3AY, +44(0)117 953 2448, www.acta-bristol.com |
Getting there Bus 24 to North Street or bus 75, 76 to West Street, then short walk | Hours
Open for productions and private hires | Tip A few hundred yards from acta on North
Street is Zara's Chocolates, a chocoholic's paradise. Watch Zara Narracott and her team
hard at work while indulging yourself in the shop-cum-cafe. You can even learn how to
make chocolate yourself at regular workshops and tasting events (www.zaraschocolates.com).

3 Alfred Fagon Statue

A trailblazing actor and playwright

Playwright, poet and actor Alfred Fagon was the first black person to have a statue put up in their honour in Bristol and it remains the only statue of a black person in the city. In June 2020, just a few days after protesters pulled down the statue of slave trader Edward Colston from its plinth in the city centre – where it had stood for 125 years – and threw it into the docks, Fagon's statue was covered in a corrosive substance which police investigated as a possible revenge attack.

Fagon was born in Jamaica in 1937, emigrated to England as a young man and lived in Bristol for many years. He died of a heart attack while jogging in London aged 49, and despite his diary and passport being in his room, the police could not find any family contacts. His body was cremated, he was given a pauper's funeral and it was three weeks before his family knew what happened. A Friends of Fagon Committee was swiftly set up to decide how to remember him. In 1987, on the first anniversary of his death, this bronze bust by David Mutasa was unveiled in St Paul's. Committee chair Paul Stephenson, who helped lead the Bristol Bus Boycott (see ch. 18), remembered Fagon as a larger-than-life character. He said at the time, 'It is hoped that the statue will inspire young people of all backgrounds to read and learn about Alfred's work and add to the artistic and cultural richness of the St Paul's community, and Bristol at large.'

After arriving in England in 1955, Fagon worked on the railways in Nottingham before joining the army and becoming a middleweight boxing champion. Back on civvy street, he travelled around the UK singing calypso before settling in Bristol, training as a welder then starting to act and write, with his plays performed on stage and on television. An annual prize now given in his memory, The Alfred Fagon Award, is the leading award for black British playwrights.

Address Grosvenor Road Triangle, St Paul's, BS2 8YA | Getting there 10-minute walk from Cabot Circus, or a stone's throw from the bus 5 stop next to the Grosvenor Road Triangle | Hours Unrestricted | Tip St Paul's Carnival takes place every year on the first Saturday in July. One of the UK's largest celebrations of African and Caribbean culture, it celebrated its 50th anniversary in 2018. Watch the colourful parade, sample amazing food and drink, and dance the night away (www.stpaulscarnival.net).

ALFRED FAGON
1937 - 1986

POET PLAYWRIGHT ACTOR

"THROUGH GRIEF TO HAPPINESS"

4 The Architecture Centre

A hub for design and the built environment

Housed in a former sail-making workshop, The Architecture Centre could easily be bypassed for the nearby Arnolfini art gallery in an old tea warehouse or the expertly made coffee from Society Cafe in an old rope factory. But do pay a visit, as it is at the heart of discussions of Bristol's past, present and future. Exhibitions often feature plans for developments across the city, and regular talks often take place in the Arnolfini's auditorium. Monthly 'ask an architect' sessions offer the chance for impartial one-on-one design consultancy.

The Architecture Centre's mission is to 'encourage the understanding and enjoyment of architecture and the wider built environment, and to champion better buildings and places for everyone'. The first organisation of its kind outside London, the registered charity hopes to appeal as much to professional architects as to those interested in shaping great places. Recent exhibitions have included discussions of affordable green homes and the creativity of children in designing a city; talks have looked at how to make Bristol a bike-friendly city, the development of the University of Bristol's new Temple Quarter Enterprise Campus (due to open in 2022) and urban farming.

Despite being based in BS1, The Architecture Centre prides itself in partnering with communities across the city, regularly working with children, young people and families in the hope of encouraging as many people as possible to get involved with their own neighbourhoods. The small Architecture Centre team is also responsible for the annual Bristol Open Doors Festival, where private buildings are opened to the public for one weekend only in September. From discovering the Avonmouth asphalt plant to the chance to climb medieval church spires, this is an invitation to explore dozens of buildings you might have walked past every day but never glimpsed inside.

Address 16 Narrow Quay, BS1 4QA, +44 (0)117 922 1540, centre@architecturecentre.org.uk, www.architecturecentre.org.uk | Getting there Short walk from city centre; a few hundred yards from m1 bus stops on Prince Street | Hours Public gallery open during exhibitions; office hours Mon–Fri 9.30am–6pm | Tip Nearby is Pero's Bridge, named in honour of Pero Jones who came to live in Bristol as the slave of John Pinney in what is now the Georgian House (www.bristolmuseums.org.uk/georgian-house-museum). A reminder of Bristol's notorious slavery past, the bridge is also well-known for the hundreds of love locks attached by smitten couples.

5 Arnos Vale Cemetery
From garden cemetery to wilderness to restoration

The Victorian businessmen who opened Arnos Vale Cemetery could never have envisaged that today, as well as continuing to hold burials and cremations, their 'garden cemetery' would also see yoga, dance classes, theatre and music in its grounds and grand chapels of rest. Visit in November and you will find a traditional Day of the Dead altar within a former crypt, featuring photographs of lost loved ones. Like this Mexican celebration, today Arnos Vale is anything but morbid thanks to a dedicated group of volunteers. In 1987 they began a campaign to secure a safe future for the site following reports that a private owner wanted to build on the grounds. A passionate citywide campaign culminated in the city council taking ownership in 2003, with Arnos Vale continuing to be a working cemetery as well as a community space. Today it is possible to explore the whole of the 45-acre estate, which provides a haven for wildlife and – if you look closely enough – has a few fairy-size doors at the base of some of its trees.

The cemetery was opened in 1839 in response to the city's old parish graveyards becoming overcrowded and something of a health hazard. The new cemetery – a private solution to a public health problem – was a grand and initially very successful scheme. Most of Bristol's leading Victorian citizens, industrialists, philanthropists, scientists and soldiers were buried here, as well as tens of thousands of others. Look out for the graves of survivors of the Charge of the Light Brigade and a police officer murdered in Old Market while trying to intervene over the ill-treatment of a donkey. Its most notable grave, however, is the social and educational reformer Raja Ram Mohan Roy, popularly known as the Father of Modern India, who died of meningitis when visiting Bristol in 1833. Repaired and conserved in 2008, his beautiful tomb is the site of an annual commemorative ceremony held on the Sunday nearest the anniversary of his death.

Address Bath Road, Brislington, BS4 3EW, +44 (0)117 971 9117, info@arnosvale.org.uk, www.arnosvale.org.uk | Getting there 20-minute walk from Bristol Temple Meads; bus 1, X 39, 57, 178 and 349 all stop outside the Bath Road gates | Hours Daily 9am – 5pm | Tip Almost directly opposite the cemetery gates is Bristol Blue Glass, where you can watch glassmakers at work in the centuries-old trade and purchase their unique pieces (www.bristol-glass.co.uk).

6 Averys
Wine from the mists of time

Stepping into Averys' historic vaulted cellars is like stepping back in time. Look out for what is affectionately known as 'the cage', where the most coveted bottles are kept. On a recent visit, Mimi Avery, the fifth generation to join the family business, unlocked the cage to reveal bottles of wine costing upwards of £600.

Averys was established on Park Street in 1793. Notable milestones include the 1850s when their centuries-old cellars were rebuilt; the 1890s when the company focused on ports and sherries; 1923, when Ronald Avery refurbished the Park Street shop featuring opulent wood panels, and fittings from the luxury transatlantic Cunard liner *Mauretania*; 1959, when Ronald trained legendary Australian winemaker Wolf Blass to blend wine; and 1966, when Averys became the first UK wine merchant to import Australian wines. These cellars under the original premises once housed their bottling line and blending tanks, and now contain their full range of more than 1000 wines. Time your visit right and you may be able to take part in a themed tasting, dine in the vaulted premises at a supper club or pop-up restaurant, or watch a movie as part of Bristol Film Festival, ideally wine-themed *Sideways*.

If wine isn't your thing, the company's 225th birthday year in 2018 saw it reintroduce its own-brand Silver Lizard gin, last bottled in the 1970s. Mimi doesn't know why the gin label she found in the archives had the name Silver Lizard, but then many things about Averys have been lost to the mists of time. In researching what this gin contained, Mimi was unable to find out what botanicals were used but did discover that it was made using the 'Bristol method', in which each botanical distilled individually. The newly recreated Averys Silver Lizard was made by Smeaton's in Oxfordshire, one of the few UK gin producers who still use the Bristol method.

Address 9A Culver Street, BS1 5LD, +44 (0)117 9214 146, www.averys.com | Getting there Short walk from the foot of Park Street or along Denmark Street from the centre | Hours Mon–Sat 10am–7pm | Tip On the side of Averys' former shop at the bottom of Park Street is the first external, moving, neon sign in Bristol, showing *Mauretania* in full steam in choppy seas. First installed in 1938, after a few years of darkness it was restored and re-illuminated in December 2018.

7 — The Bag of Nails

The cat pub

Come to the Bag of Nails for its constantly changing selection of beers, its vinyl records, Lego nights, Tuesday evening quiz and the musings of landlord Luke Daniels – winner of the Beard Liberation Society's beard of the year 2015. Those in the know also get a beer from here before taking it to the fantastic Indian restaurant Chai Shai just a few doors down.

Don't come to this small pub if you don't like cats, because it's big on them. If you do like cats, though, and you correctly time your visit, you will be in for a treat, with at least one family of furry felines often to be found either taking a nap on the bar among the hand pulls or wandering around among the legs of the customers – who still popped in one at a time for takeaway beer during the coronavirus pandemic of 2020. One might even be found relaxing on a cat-sized chaise longue as a vinyl record spins on a player in one corner. Camera phones are often at the ready to get an Instagramable picture of the cute creatures curled up among the splendid choices of beer, but regulars think nothing of the cats – although many still love a good stroke (or 'smooth', to use Bristolian vernacular). The cats are now very much part of the furniture of the pub, and just as some of the regulars ignore them, they often completely ignore their human company. Walk by when the Bag of Nails isn't open and a cat might be fast asleep on the windowsill at the front. Stroll along one of the paths in nearby Brandon Hill and you might see one on an expedition.

When you're here, whether surrounded by cats or not, keep an eye out for the two dozen or so rules from Luke handwritten on a pillar. Number 2: 'Daily Mail opinions will have the piss taken out of them'. Number 5: 'No Scientology'. Number 9: 'No stiletto heels on my floor'. There are also no dogs or children allowed. Cats, however, are very much welcome.

Address 141 St George's Road, BS1 5UW | **Getting there** 5-minute walk from College Green | **Hours** Daily noon–11pm | **Tip** If felines are your thing, head to Bristol's only cat cafe, You & Meow on Denmark Street. Pay to spend one or two hours in the company of these purrfect companions (www.youandmeow.co.uk).

8 __ The Balmoral

Hoping for new nautical adventures

The *Balmoral* is the UK's most widely travelled excursion ship, having visited more British ports than any other vessel – carrying more than two million passengers around the coastlines of Britain, Ireland and northern France. But the historic pleasure cruiser has been tied up in Bristol's docks since 2017 with a bid of almost £4 million recently submitted to the Heritage Lottery Fund for urgent repairs to enable it to sail again.

The 62-metre craft was commissioned in 1949 as a replacement for a paddle steamer of the same name, providing a passenger ferry service from Southampton to the Isle of Wight. Car ferries put paid to its original purpose and it later undertook trips to resorts along the Bristol Channel, narrowly avoiding becoming a floating restaurant and disco in Dundee, before calling Bristol its home port from 1986. In recent years, however, it has featured in more films than it has undertaken voyages, with the ship and numerous other Bristol locations spottable in both *Stan & Ollie* and *The Guernsey Literary & Potato Peel Pie Society*. Its current lack of nautical adventures is due to new regulations from the Maritime & Coastal Agency, which stipulates that double plates in the hull and a lack of fireproofing in the crew accommodation mean it is no longer suitable for sailing.

For many years, training ship HMS *Flying Fox* was moored close to where the *Balmoral* is today. The Royal Navy Reserve Training Centre on Winterstoke Road near Ashton Gate Stadium is still called HMS Flying Fox after the ship. Another former Navy vessel – originally the HMS *Messina* – is still moored nearby, now called the *Pride of Bristol* and providing opportunities for young people to experience life at sea in the Bristol Channel. Despite the *Balmoral* not moving from its current berth, a committed team of volunteers keeps the boat shipshape and Bristol fashion, with the brass fittings as gleaming today as they were when the ship was built in Liverpool more than 70 years ago.

Address Hotwell Road, Hotwells, BS8 4UJ, www.mvbalmoral.org | Getting there Numerous buses to Hotwell Road; Bristol Ferry Boats or No. 7 ferry to Mardyke Ferry Landing | Hours Exterior always visible, only open to the public during the annual Bristol Open Doors festival (www.bristolopendoors.org.uk) | Tip Kyle Blue is Bristol's only floating hostel, with private and shared sleeping cabins, a lounge, and self-catering kitchen on a boat moored close to Wapping Wharf (www.kylebluebristol.co.uk).

9 Barton Hill Settlement

A vital community resource

The charitable beginnings of Barton Hill Settlement could soon be coming full circle. Founded by the University of Bristol in 1911 so that university staff and students could live there and spread enlightenment, it has been described as 'a radically liberal community', with much of its early activities focusing on reducing the area's high infant mortality rate. During World War I it provided an important source of support for women whose men were away fighting or who had become widowed, later supporting campaigns such as votes for women and helping to feed the families of local workers when they went on strike.

Now a vital resource for local residents and visitors alike, offering everything from support for the over-50s to summer picnics, around 50 community groups meet here. It is also home to the likes of Bristol's Somali Resource Centre and Travelling Light Theatre Company. A visit can also not take place without popping into the cafe, where a slice of cake costs just 20p and owner Maggie seems to know all of her customers by name – within a space that in 2020 was in the process of changing its name from Barton Hill Settlement to Wellspring Settlement.

In 2019, *The Guardian* newspaper was criticised for a headline saying that the University of Bristol was expanding to the 'wrong side of the tracks'. Joanna Holmes, CEO of the Barton Hill Settlement, called the university 'symbolically posh'. Talking about its proposed new campus a short distance from Barton Hill, Joanna said: 'This new campus feels like the university coming down the hill to the rest of us.' The university has not had anything to do with Barton Hill since the 1970s, but within a new 'micro-settlement', it is planning to teach students within converted shipping containers, with tiny bedsits above for people who want to study but need a place with a stable low rent to make that possible.

Address 43 Ducie Road, Barton Hill, BS5 0AX, +44 (0)117 955 6971,
www.bartonhillsettlement.org.uk | **Getting there** A few minutes' walk from bus 36 stop
on Queen Ann Road and also Lawrence Hill railway station; within easy cycling distance
of the Bristol & Bath Railway Path | **Hours** Mon 9am–5pm, Tue–Thu 9am–9pm,
Sat & Sun 9am–5pm | **Tip** Walk through Netham Park to reach Netham Locks, the
upstream entrance to the Feeder Canal and Floating Harbour. The canal diverts water
from the River Avon, thus maintaining a constant water level in the harbour. The lock
remains in regular use and is overlooked by a lock-keeper's house and toll house.

10 The Bearpit

The travails of a sunken roundabout

The Bearpit was the creation of Bristol's city planners of the 1960s, who swept wide roads straight through historic neighbourhoods. A lot of property was destroyed, a huge hole was dug for a pedestrian concourse . . . but neither the roads nor the underpass materialised. It was never meant to look like this. A similar story happened in Totterdown, another neighbourhood split in half for a road that never came. The ultimate symbol of this devastation is the M32, cutting a cruel swathe through the communities of Easton and St Paul's.

Officially named St James Barton Roundabout after the land on which it was built, its adopted name might have been given by street cleaners who thought its layout resembled sunken bearpits at zoos. By the 2010s, many considered it a no-go area because of anti-social behaviour. For others, however, this was what made it so attractive: an area seemingly outside the law, where creativity flourished. A further problem was establishing who curated its activities. The People's Republic of Stokes Croft (see ch. 96) erected a bear sculpture called *Ursa* and an open-air theatre. The Bearpit Improvement Group converted a double-decker bus into a restaurant, and shipping containers into a cafe and shop.

In 2018, Bristol City Council decided that enough was enough. 'A lot has been achieved,' said deputy mayor Asher Craig. 'But we cannot ignore the unacceptable anti-social behaviour that has taken place recently, so it is necessary for us to take action and take back full control of the area. We need to ensure that this space is providing a safe and positive environment that people across the city can enjoy.' So, what for the future? Ideas have included a multi-million-pound 'food innovation hub' called The Circle. But as of 2020, those plans appeared to have been shelved, with the Bearpit remaining a tantalisingly blank canvas.

Address St James Barton Roundabout, BS1 3LE | Getting there 2-minute walk from Bristol bus station; 2-minute walk from Stokes Croft | Hours Unrestricted | Tip On Bond Street overlooking the Bearpit is a sculpture by Paul Mount called *The Spirit of Bristol*. Commissioned in 1968, the 20-foot-high work in stainless steel features sails representing Bristol's maritime heritage and an aerofoil similar to that of Concorde to signify the city's aviation links.

11 Beese's

Messing about on the river

Nestled beside a picturesque, wooded stretch of the River Avon, Beese's was founded in 1846 by Anne Beese to provide refreshments to travellers and workers using or crossing the river. Despite appearing not to have changed for centuries, this area was once home to a dozen small quarries, with coal and pennant sandstone transported by horse-drawn barges to Bristol and Bath. It's hard to believe now, enjoying a cream tea at Beese's, that there also used to be a sewage works and refuse tip nearby.

The ferry connecting Beese's to the Hanham side of the Avon is the oldest continuously operating service across the river. The best way to arrive at this tea rooms and bar is undoubtedly by boat, either by hailing the ferry from the opposite footpath or making the longer journey from Bristol city centre via Bristol Ferry Boats, Bristol Packet or Number Seven Boat Trips services. Many of the regular ferry trips include food at Beese's in the price of the ticket.

Until recently, cream teas were the order of the day here. These continue to be popular but there is now an expanded food menu that also includes salads and a Sunday roast. Despite being less than three miles from Temple Meads, this area really does feel like the middle of the countryside. City life winks at you when, from the garden and decked area, you can sometimes hear and spot a train as it makes a brief appearance between the tunnels of St Anne's and Broomhill. In 2020, a seal even swam this far up the river from the Bristol Channel.

Bristol is well known for its bars and restaurants on the water – think the Grain Barge in Hotwells, and Under the Stars and Fish in the city centre. There's even the Thekla, a floating live-music venue on board a ship that once transported timber around the Baltic Sea. But Beese's has got a special charm all of its own, and there's never any need to hurry when arriving by boat.

Address Wyndham Crescent, St Anne's, BS4 4SX, +44 (0)117 977 7412, info@beeses.co.uk, www.beeses.co.uk | Getting there Conham Ferry costs £1 per person to Beese's from Conham River Park; bus 1 stops nearby; several ferry services from city centre | Hours Fri & Sat noon–11pm, Sun & bank holiday Mon noon–7pm | Tip A couple of miles upstream on the other side of the river is the Old Lock & Weir. The traditional cider house with a riverside terrace next to Hanham Lock features in Arthur Conan Doyle's 1889 novel *Micah Clarke* (www.lockandweir.com).

12 The Black Castle

A weird and wonderful folly

How did a pub disguised as a castle end up in the middle of a supermarket car park? To answer this question, we must go back to when this area was still all fields in the early 18th century and then purchased by a wealthy copper smelter. What is now the Black Castle pub within the grounds of Sainsbury's was built in the 1740s to house stables, offices and 'pleasure rooms' for a grand home, Mount Pleasant, now Arnos Court Hotel. Its blackness comes from the unusual materials this weird and wonderful folly was built from: the walls are made of black copper-slag blocks recycled from copper smelting works at nearby Crew's Hole.

When the writer Horace Walpole arrived in Brislington in 1766 on a journey to Bristol, he was left aghast by the 'large Gothic building, coal black and striped with white. I took it for the Devil's Cathedral!' Look out for the head of King Henry VIII on its exterior, alongside crenellated parapets, fake arrow slits and turrets. Many of the freestone carvings and dressings are believed to come from Bristol's demolished medieval gateways and from St Werburgh's Church when it was still located on Corn Street. Hidden from public view, there is a former chapel on the second floor of the main tower. Other internal decorations such as carved heads can still be glimpsed on the ground floor within the pub.

In the 1940s and 1950s, the castle was used as the Bristol Tramways Sport & Social Club, with Bristol City Council's fleet services team still operating from the neighbouring Sandy Park depot just the other side of the pub from Arno's Court Triumphal Arch, some of whose carvings are also thought to come from the medieval city walls. Owned by Greene King for almost a decade, a new landlord took on the Black Castle in the summer of 2019, promising to restore it to its former glory. We're sure that he doesn't mean converting it back into stables.

Address St Philip's Causeway, Brislington, BS4 3BD, +44 (0)117 977 8720, www.greeneking-pubs.co.uk/pubs/avon/castle | Getting there 20-minute walk from Temple Meads; bus 1, X39 or 349 to the Burger King on Bath Road – pub is opposite | Hours Daily 11am–11pm | Tip Lost & Grounded are on a mission to dispel the myths about lager being an inferior style of beer. Try Keller Pils, their signature drink, in their St Anne's brewery that hosts special events throughout the year (www.lostandgrounded.co.uk).

13 Boiling Wells

The clue is in the name

As with Hotwells to the west of the city centre, it doesn't take a linguistics scholar to arrive at the derivation of Boiling Wells in St Werburgh's. While we're on the subject of etymology, St Werburgh's itself is named after the church that was rebuilt like a giant Lego set after being transported brick by brick from Corn Street. The church still stands on Mina Road but is now a climbing centre close to Mina Road tunnel (see ch. 70).

Boiling Wells was once the source of springs whose bubbling resembled boiling water. The water was powerful but never hot, with a pipe known as the Quay Pipe constructed as early as the 13th century to transport fresh water from here to the quay on St Augustine's Reach almost two miles away, to supply both citizens and ships. It is probable that John Cabot's ships that set sail from Bristol in 1476 and discovered Newfoundland took water from the Quay Pipe on their historic voyage. By 1880, the pipe had been diverted to supply water from Boiling Wells to the Bristol United Brewery on Lewins Mead. The old ironworks of the Quay Pipe, which was eventually destroyed in 1936, are now on display at the Bristol Water museum in Blagdon.

Thanks to Boiling Wells' pure waters, watercress was once commercially harvested close to the source and still grows wild despite the spring no longer bubbling, with nearby Watercress Road a reminder of this part of the area's history. Today, 2.5 acres of Boiling Wells, with wild green spaces, a terraced orchard and outdoor amphitheatre, form part of St Werburgh's City Farm (see ch. 91). The site is used during the week for outdoor activities, often supporting vulnerable children and adults. It really comes alive for the farm's seasonal celebrations such as a traditional West Country wassail where the apple trees are blessed to ensure a good crop. Expect mulled cider, live music, food, drink, storytelling and family fun.

Address Boiling Wells Lane, St Werburgh's, BS2 9XY | **Getting there** An adventure in itself. Bus 5 to James Street by The Victoria pub, and walk up Mina Road and Boiling Wells Lane through a small tunnel under the railway line. From the other direction, bus 17 or 24 to Muller Road, walk down footpath by school playing fields towards Watercress Farm. | **Hours** Boiling Wells Lane is a public highway. The farm's Boiling Wells site is open on some weekends and for seasonal celebrations. | **Tip** Every home in The Yard off Boiling Wells Lane was individually designed and built by their owner on what was a scaffolding yard. Also here, the Wild Goose Space hosts everything from mother and baby yoga to pop-up restaurants (www.wildgoosespace.org.uk).

14 Bottle Yard Studios
The Hollywood of the South West

Broadchurch, Hellboy, Poldark, Sherlock, The Crystal Maze. If a television series or movie has filmed in Bristol in recent years, chances are that the Bottle Yard Studios were involved. Operating for more than 50 years as a winery and bottling plant, the Bottle Yard is now one of the UK's largest dedicated film and TV studio facilities, with Stephanie Marshall, regional head of the BBC, recently saying that Bristol 'has truly become the Hollywood of the South West'. Thanks to its workshops, production offices, costume and dressing rooms, and on-site tenants providing a variety of industry services, the Bottle Yard – owned by Bristol City Council and until 2020 under the inspirational leadership of Fiona Francombe – is often used as a base for productions filming in the region.

In 2017, Bristol was designated a UNESCO City of Film in recognition of the city's achievements as a world leader in the field of film and the moving image, joining the likes of Rome, Sofia and Sydney in holding this accolade. 'Lights, camera, action' is a familiar refrain, and spotting both big-screen and small-screen locations is a popular pastime for Bristolians. Wasn't that Broad Street doubling as 1960s' London in *The Trial of Christine Keeler*? Was Hellboy strolling down the corridors of a block of flats in Redcliffe? Were those really Daleks on the Clifton Suspension Bridge?

One of the Bottle Yard's big selling points is its enormity. It boasts eight stages, whose largest floor area measures 21,700 square feet (2,020 square metres) and the largest roof height 65 feet (20 metres) – perfect for the requirements of big productions. The team behind ABC's Emmy-nominated *Galavant* constructed medieval castle sets in a space that for decades stored millions of gallons of drinks, including Harveys Bristol Cream sherry, before they were transported across the globe. Now, instead of drinks sent worldwide, it is the sights and sounds of Bristol via television and film.

Address Whitchurch Lane, Hengrove, BS14 0BH, +44(0)117 357 6888, thebottleyard@bristol.gov.uk, www.thebottleyard.com | **Getting there** Bus 75, 92 or m1 to Hengrove Park; visitor parking onsite | **Hours** Studios open to the public only during Bristol Open Doors festival (www.bristolopendoors.org.uk); Reel Café open Mon–Fri 8am–3pm | **Tip** In nearby Hengrove Park are the remains of the main runway of the original Bristol Airport, where thrill-seekers were once able to pay a few shillings for a short pleasure flight. The sole civilian airport open during World War II, it closed in 1957 when the new Bristol Airport was opened in Lulsgate.

15 Brandy Bottom Colliery

A rare example of a largely forgotten industry

Coal mining was once a key industry in Bristol, with coal fields – some only a few miles from the city centre – providing fuel to heat homes and power expanding industries. Coal was first dug in Kingswood to the east of the city, and throughout the 19th century many of the region's green spaces were gradually occupied by collieries with their associated engine houses, winding gear and a maze of shafts sometimes stretching to 300 metres deep.

Thanks to sitting on coal seams, the small town of Bedminster grew into a large suburb of Bristol with more than 70,000 inhabitants by 1884. At its peak, Bedminster's Dean Lane Colliery – now a skate park and street art hotspot – employed more than 400 men and some children. The men were paid £2 to £3 per week and the children sometimes as little as 4d per day at a mine where there was an average of one fatal accident per month. Bristol's coal industry declined in the late 1800s and now few traces remain, making Brandy Bottom Colliery even more important. South Liberty Lane Pit in Ashton Vale (where Bristol City FC once had plans to build their new stadium) was the last Bristol coal mine to close, in 1925, and pubs such as the Miners Arms in St Werburgh's recall the largely forgotten industry.

Brandy Bottom Colliery is a 19th-century steam-powered colliery located on the South Gloucestershire coalfield which opened around 1837 as Lord Radnor's Pit. Acquired at auction by the East Bristol Collieries company in 1900, it is thought that coal hoisting here ceased sometime before World War I. It was made a Scheduled Ancient Monument in 2001 and today consists of two groups of derelict buildings, plus a number of other features such as spoil heaps, that together form a rare example of the surface layout of a 19th-century colliery. It is one of the best-preserved Victorian examples in the UK.

Address Coxgrove Hill, Pucklechurch, Gloucestershire, BS16 9NL, www.aibt.org/
brandy-bottom.html | **Getting there** Just a few hundred yards south of where the Bristol
& Bath Railway Path crosses Coxgrove Hill | **Hours** Guided tours and work parties
take place throughout the year | **Tip** Named after Lord Radnor, the Radnor Hotel on
St Nicholas Street was from the early 1940s Bristol's first gay pub, two decades before
homosexuality was legalised in 1967. The building is now a lovingly renovated events
space (www.theradnorrooms.co.uk).

16 Bristol & Bath Railway Path

A daily pedal rather than a daily grind

What was once the Midland Railway line connecting Bristol and Bath is now a popular car-free cycling and walking route, as well as being a green corridor through inner-city Bristol. The railway line was closed at the end of the 1960s, with the track bed of the former line becoming a path which today is used by more people on two wheels and two feet than it was by passengers during the days of steam. The Bristol & Bath Railway Path (also known as the cycle path or just 'the path') starts in St Philip's through an archway which sees metal girders skilfully fashioned into tree trunks, branches and leaves: a perfect visual metaphor for the path. It's not the only artwork along the 13-mile route either. Keep a lookout for an upside-down fish made out of bricks and balanced on its nose, a sculpture of a drinking giant, and mosaics within tunnels telling the story of the local areas.

Constructed by hundreds of volunteers between 1979 and 1986, the path was the very first part of the UK's National Cycle Network. Today it is used by thousands of commuters as well as families walking to school and runners out for a jog. At its busiest times it can be somewhat spoiled by inconsiderate cyclists looking to beat their Strava personal bests. But that lessens neither its beauty nor its usefulness; every journey offers a chance for peace and reflection away from the daily grind. Cycling along the path is often the quickest and definitely the most fun way to travel from the city centre to areas including Easton, Redcliffe and Kingswood. And at the weekend or during the holidays, cycling its full length to Bath is eminently achievable for even the youngest pedallers. Along the way, you will pass the former Elizabeth Shaw chocolate factory, popular outdoor swimming spots and the Avon Valley Railway in Bitton, where you may glimpse a working steam train.

Address Path starts at corner of St Philip's Road and Trinity Street through Newtown Park, St Philip's, BS2 0AJ, www.bristolbathrailwaypath.org.uk | **Getting there** Only a few minutes' cycle ride from Bristol Temple Meads | **Hours** Unrestricted | **Tip** How about walking or cycling along the railway path between stops during the biannual East Bristol Brewery Trail? Six breweries welcome visitors to sample their wares, often accompanied by delicious grub from local street food traders (www.eastbristolbrewerytrail.com).

17 __ Bristol Bike Project

Love on two wheels

From repairing bicycles in a back garden in Montpelier, The Bristol Bike Project has evolved since being founded in 2008 into a thriving charity working with more than 50 local organisations. Their objectives remain unchanged: to empower underprivileged and marginalised people whose lives would be greatly improved by sustainable transportation; to provide a vibrant and supportive workshop environment; to promote skill-sharing and independence; and to divert and redirect functional bicycles and their working parts from recycling and landfill.

The idea for the project came after a cycling trip around Norway by co-founders Colin Fan and James Lucas, who while volunteering at Bristol Refugee Rights had seen the importance for asylum seekers to be independently mobile. With public transport and car ownership beyond many of them, in a city already overly reliant on fossil fuels, the objective to help people get out on two wheels became crystal clear. The pair were soon inundated with unwanted bicycles, and endeavoured to get them out to as many deserving folk as possible. Fast-forward to the present and The Bristol Bike Project has not just expanded its workshop space but become a community interest company with a trading arm to help sustainably fund their charitable work. At their premises around the back of Hamilton House on Stokes Croft, you might find a workshop for socially isolated adults; an unemployed young person learning basic repair skills by working with a mechanic to refurbish a donated bike; or a friendly, informal workshop for women sharing knowledge.

When you visit, don't just have a look. Get stuck in! Fix your own bike at one of their workshops, sign up for a maintenance course or volunteer to help others get out on two wheels. The team also offers tours to help people set up their own similar bike projects in a different town or city.

Address Hamilton House, 7 City Road, St Paul's, BS2 8TN, +44 (0)117 942 1794, www.thebristolbikeproject.org, hello@thebristolbikeproject.org | Getting there 10-minute walk from Montpelier station; bus 5 to City Road outside The Bristol Bike Project; numerous buses to Stokes Croft or Cheltenham Road | Hours Mon–Fri 9am–6pm, Sat 10.30am–5.30pm | Tip Across the street from Bristol Bike Project is Idle Hands, one of the city's few remaining record shops. As well as stocking an unrivalled collection of vinyl from breakbeat to reggae, owner Chris Farrell is the man in the know as to what's happening in Bristol's music scene (www.idlehandsbristol.com).

18 Bristol Bus Boycott

A watershed moment for UK civil rights

It may not have the same global recognition as Martin Luther King's peaceful protests in the United States, but a bus boycott in Bristol modelled on the civil rights struggle across the pond had a profound effect and proved to be a crucial step on the road towards the UK's first laws against racial discrimination.

The Bristol Bus Boycott of 1963 began after 18-year-old Guy Bailey was turned away from a job interview at the state-owned Bristol Omnibus Company, being told by a manager that they did not employ black people. The practice, which was entirely legal at the time, led to a boycott of the city's entire bus network, inspired by the actions of Rosa Parks, who had refused to give up her seat to a white passenger in the USA. After four months of pickets, blockades and sit-down protests on bus routes throughout the city, the company relented. They declared a change in policy to complete integration for all employees on the same day as King's 'I have a dream' speech in Washington DC. Raghbir Singh was the first person to break the colour bar when the ban was lifted, becoming a bus conductor. Just two years after the Bristol Bus Boycott, Harold Wilson's Labour government passed the UK's first Race Relations Act.

The colourful commemorative plaque in the bus station was unveiled in 2014 by Bailey alongside his fellow bus boycott campaigners Paul Stephenson and Roy Hackett. Historian David Olusoga recently chose the boycott in his top-ten list for Historic England's 'History of England in 100 Places' campaign, on the theme of the history of power, protest and progress. 'In the context of the times this was an incredibly important and dignified protest, carefully linked to the wider civil rights struggle,' said Olusoga, also the presenter of BBC Two's *A House Through Time* which in its third series in 2020 focused on the history of 10 Guinea Street in Redcliffe.

Address Bristol Bus & Coach Station, Marlborough Street, BS1 3NU | Getting there Easiest by bus, or a 3-minute walk from Stokes Croft | Hours Unrestricted | Tip Next door to the bus station is St James' Priory, the oldest building in Bristol, founded in c. 1134 as a cell of the Benedictine Abbey of Tewkesbury. Catch a glimpse of the church from inside Cafe Refectoire, whose profits support the charitable work of St James' Priory (www.stjamespriory.org.uk).

19 Bristol Castle

Still visible if you look closely

Once the beating heart of Bristol, with bustling shopping streets, homes, schools and theatres, Castle Park was almost completely destroyed by the Luftwaffe during the 1940–1941 Bristol Blitz. Nine hundred years before, it was home to Bristol Castle. The largest Norman castle in England when it was built in the 11th century, it was demolished in the mid-1600s. Now only a few crumbling walls and underground chambers remain. The first mention of a castle in Bristol is in the *Anglo-Saxon Chronicle* of 1088. The original structure was most likely a timber tower built on a raised mound (motte) enclosed by a courtyard (bailey), in turn surrounded by a protective ditch and high timber fence. In the early 1100s, Robert, First Earl of Gloucester levelled the motte and rebuilt the keep in stone. Vestiges can still be seen today, merging with the remains of Victorian brickwork from the Llewellins & James brass foundry that occupied the site until the Blitz.

The best-preserved parts of the castle surviving above ground are the vaulted chambers, a series of interconnecting carved stone arches over two rooms. Probably once the entrance to the castle's great hall, the building might soon be brought back into use. In 2019, Paul Smith, Bristol City Council cabinet member for housing, tweeted that the chambers could become a cafe or restaurant. A sally port, once a hidden castle entrance originally accessed via an underground tunnel that allowed the castle's defenders to attack besiegers, can be accessed during Bristol Open Doors festival. Walk down steps only rediscovered during archaeological excavations in the early 1970s, which also unearthed a monkey skeleton. The only other remnant of the castle is a portion of the 12th-century south curtain wall containing a slit window for archers defending the River Avon approach. Unfortunately, no archers now protect it from graffiti.

Address Castle Park, BS1 3XB | **Getting there** Arrive by ferry (Bristol Ferry Boats or No. 7) at Castle Park landing stage; 10-minute walk from Bristol Temple Meads; numerous nearby bus stops | **Hours** Unrestricted | **Tip** Cross from Castle Park to Finzels Reach over Castle Bridge for a drink at Left Handed Giant Brewpub. The brewery raised more than one million pounds to open their splendid new premises in 2019 (www.lhgbrewpub.com).

20 Bristol Cathedral Garden

A small oasis of calm

Unlike those of other English cities, Bristol's cathedral does not dominate its skyline. The Augustinian abbey became a cathedral in 1542 and is actually one of two in the city, the other being the Catholic Cathedral Church of Saints Peter and Paul up in Clifton (also known as Clifton Cathedral). Walk through Bristol Cathedral, through the cloister rebuilt in the 15th century and the cafe built in 1969, push open a door and find yourself in its garden, a secret oasis of calm nestled in the city centre. The sound of birdsong is accompanied by the low rumble of traffic from Anchor Road below. It is easy to forget how close the city is when sitting on a bench in the garden or taking a lunchtime stroll among its treasures. (Just be sure to watch out for exposed tree roots.)

The garden is currently maintained by four volunteers from the cathedral congregation, who in recent years have undertaken much pruning and restoration work. A holly bush has been fashioned into the shape of a cross, three imposing plane trees form a border at the garden's southern edge and graves dating back hundreds of years – some so worn that it is impossible to read their inscriptions – can be found among lavender, ferns and witch hazel. In one corner, a sundial bears the name of John Bentley Freeman, who died aged only 20 in the Battle of the Menin Road during World War One, with his father Herbert – a canon of Bristol Cathedral – and mother Ida also remembered.

In another corner, a small herb garden is a reminder of when herbs were cultivated both for medicinal and culinary use in medieval monastery gardens. Traditional herbs planted here include fennel, lovage, feverfew and marjoram. With this being a cathedral garden, plants in flower are organised by the Ecclesiastical year such as hellebores, skimmia and hamamelis at Christmas, and daffodils, geraniums and tulips at Easter.

Address College Green, BS1 5TJ, www.bristol-cathedral.co.uk | Getting there Unmissable on College Green, served by plenty of buses | Hours Accessible during cathedral opening hours | Tip As well as services, the cathedral plays host to a variety of events throughout the year, including music concerts, film screenings and even dinners in the nave.

21 Bristol Central Library

Books in breathtaking spaces

Bristol's original library – the second-earliest public municipal library in England – was opened in 1613 on King Street, was rebuilt a century later and is now a Chinese restaurant. In 1901, after £50,000 was set aside in a design competition for a new Bristol Library, the firm of H. Percy Adams won with designs by his 27-year-old assistant Charles Holden, who created the exterior of the building in a blend of styles, and inside employed large arches and high ceilings, creating some breathtaking spaces. *Pevsner's Architectural Guide to Bristol* by Andrew Foyle describes how the precocious Holden drew on 'mathematical logic, spatial manipulation and Arts and Crafts respect for locale – while synthesising a new and infinitely pleasing design'.

Walk up the stairs nearest to College Green and find yourself in the grand marble-clad vestibule, with domes tiled in turquoise mosaics. The rest of the ground floor is more functional, containing a cafe and children's section, so head upstairs and walk along a low vaulted corridor towards the reading room. The books in its upper gallery are accessed by spiral staircases. Also upstairs is the Bristol Room, which contains the library's oldest books and was designed to house fittings from the reference room of the original King Street library, including wood panelling, bookcases and furniture. Stay to the end of the working day in its replacement and experience the sight of a member of library staff walking around the building while ringing a loud bell, indicating that it is time to leave.

In these times of austerity, local authorities must find ways to make money, and in 2013 Bristol City Council leased Central Library's lower ground floor and basement to Bristol Cathedral Choir School, allowing their new primary school to move in, with glass-block panels in the library floor helping to illuminate the lower levels.

Address Deanery Road, BS1 5TL, +44(0)117 903 7250, www.bristol.gov.uk/libraries | Getting there A stone's throw from College Green | Hours Mon, Wed & Fri 9.30am–5pm, Tue & Thu 9.30am–7pm, Sat 10am–5pm, Sun 1–5pm | Tip Holden incorporated the mid-12th-century Abbey Gatehouse next door into his building. It was once the main entrance to the Augustinian abbey precinct, now part of Bristol Cathedral and Bristol Cathedral Choir School.

22 Bristol County Ground

Reflecting cricket's place in the city

A cricketing colossus once bestrode Bristol County Ground. W. G. Grace did more than any other man to help found the modern game, and for many people is the biggest celebrity ever to have come out of Bristol. Grace was born in 1848 and captained both Gloucestershire and England. Nets where he used to practise can still be found in The Old England pub in Montpelier, with two other pubs – The W. G. Grace on Whiteladies Road and the Grace on Gloucester Road – named in his memory. There is also a blue plaque at 15 Victoria Square in Clifton where he once lived.

A mural of W. G. is part of colourful renovations of the County Ground which took place in 2019 when Gloucestershire were promoted to Division One of the County Championship ahead of their 150th anniversary season in 2020. W. G. lining up a red security light doubling as a cricket ball features in a two-storey mural on the side of one building, and also as part of a walk of legends who have been immortalised on pillars at the Ashley Down end of the ground. Graffiti artist Silent Hobo was commissioned by the club to paint a series of murals; they start with a huge yellow cricket ball and club crest bursting out of a wall near the Nevil Road entrance. The Clifton Suspension Bridge features in another mural further on, alongside a few cricketers and other landmarks including Ashton Court mansion, with hot air balloons and Concorde overhead.

Above the new street art, Bristol County Ground's 45-metre-high floodlights installed in 2016 have been referred to as giant spatulas and can be seen from across the city. But despite their detractors, they mean that the club can now host day-night cricket matches including international games, as well as music events which in recent years have seen the likes of Elton John and Tom Jones grace the outfield where the great W. G. once ruled supreme.

Address Nevil Road, Ashley Down, BS7 9EJ, +44(0)117 910 8017, tickets@glosccc.co.uk, www.gloscricket.co.uk | **Getting there** Numerous buses run within a 5-minute walk of the main entrance | **Hours** Check website for fixture list | **Tip** Next door is a new museum celebrating the work of George Müller, who built five orphanages in Bristol, caring for and educating 10,000 young people between 1836 and his death in 1898 (www.mullers.org/museum).

23 Bristol Improv Theatre
The UK's first venue dedicated to improv

Bristol is the city where the world's first bungee jump took place from the Clifton Suspension Bridge, where women first sat on a jury and where Ribena was tasted for the first time having been invented at the former National Fruit & Cider Institute in nearby Long Ashton. A more recent first to add is the opening in 2018 of the Bristol Improv Theatre, the first of its kind in the UK. ('Improv' is short for 'improvisation', and improv actors create plays without scripts by listening and responding to each other. This makes every show completely unique and often very exciting.)

After using venues across the city for their shows, a successful crowdfunding campaign raised £27,000 for the first phase of renovations to the former Polish Ex-Servicemen's Club in Clifton, building a 120-seat theatre, rehearsal rooms, bar and office space. Calling themselves 'the spiritual home' of spontaneous and interactive theatre and comedy in the South West, this social enterprise and not-for-profit organisation is proud to support the UK's growing improvised theatre and comedy scene. 'We exist to produce original work and programming, spread the word about our increasingly popular art form, and make people's lives more fun through the practice of improv,' say the founders.

The Bristol Improv Theatre promotes improvised drama, musical theatre and storytelling as well as comedy. Regular events include Theatre Jam, a weekly performance and social night; and The Bish Bash Bosh, pitting feisty improvisers from Team Bish against Team Bosh. The venue is also regularly hired out by the likes of Bristol Bad Film Club and Bristol Burlesque Festival. And if you would like to learn how to improvise, the theatre holds a regular six-week discovering-improv class. After completing the course, you too could be improvising with the best of them on the Bristol Improv Theatre stage.

Address 50 St Paul's Road, Clifton, BS8 1LP, +44 (0)7936 617158, hello@improvtheatre.co.uk, www.improvtheatre.co.uk | Getting there Bus 8 or 9 to Queen's Road; 15-minute walk from Clifton Down station | Hours Hours vary depending on shows. Keep an eye on their website and social media channels. | Tip Just a short walk from Bristol Improv Theatre is the luxurious Lido, featuring an outdoor swimming pool, spa, cafe and restaurant. Look out for their Swim & Eat packages from £35 per person (www.lidobristol.com).

24 BWRP

Transforming waste into shared assets

A giant handsaw the length of a minibus can be found above one wall of Bristol Wood Recycling Project. Of course it's made out of wood – just one of the inventive uses for salvaged timber that this much-loved social enterprise has been part of over the last 15 years. In that time, BWRP has sold and reused waste wood diverted from landfill, saving more than 5,000 tonnes of wood and in turn providing Bristol's trade, domestic, creative and alternative communities with a fantastic and affordable resource. Staff and volunteers hand-sort and de-nail waste wood, allowing each useful piece a new lease of life through BWRP's timber yard and workshop. Through one door comes old wood; it might leave another transformed into furniture. Timber which cannot be reused is recycled into woodchip, or made into logs or kindling.

The outlook continues to be bright for BWRP but its future looked dicey in 2017 when they were forced to leave their home of more than a decade on land next to Temple Meads as work began to prepare for the University of Bristol's new campus. Fortunately, new premises were located less than a mile away, enabling BWRP to expand their growing business of reusing and recycling waste wood, building furniture, and offering employment and volunteering opportunities. Their new, larger site has two entrance points, enabling separate access for collections and clients, as well as a self-contained yard for storing waste wood. The workshop is now more than twice the size of the one on the old premises, and also located conveniently close to Bristol City Council's household waste recycling centre.

During its time developing a self-financing business model, BWRP has grown from a simple idea into a significant enterprise with a dozen paid employees and a substantial social and environmental impact, becoming an essential part of Bristol's alternative economic identity.

Address Unit 4, William Street, St Philip's, BS2 0RG, +44 (0)117 329 4319, woodshop@bwrp.org.uk, www.bwrp.org.uk | Getting there 5-minute walk from Temple Meads | Hours Mon–Fri 9am–5pm, Sat 10am–4pm | Tip Good Chemistry, across the street, has swiftly become one of Bristol's best-respected breweries since its founding in 2015. Visit their brewery tap on William Street on Fridays and Saturdays between April and September, or their award-winning pub, The Good Measure, on Chandos Road in Redland (www.goodchemistrybrewing.co.uk).

25 __ Broadmead Baptist Church

The church above the shops

Thousands of shoppers pass by Broadmead Baptist Church every day, unaware that it even exists, but a church has stood here since a chapel was founded on this site in 1640. The area survived heavy World War II bombing before being redeveloped in the 1960s, replacing what is now Castle Park as the city's main shopping district. Today, Broadmead remains busy with shoppers and visitors to its popular annual German Christmas market. Look up while you walk down Union Street and you will see Broadmead Baptist Church – known as 'the church above the shops'. Completed in 1969, it has a spacious timber-clad interior within a Brutalist concrete shell; without its original timber spire it is even more hidden from view.

Broadmead's first Baptist worshippers were initially persecuted by the civil and established church authorities, but despite this the church grew steadily in numbers during the 17th century. Significant Broadmead worshippers over the centuries include William Knibb, who campaigned successfully against slavery in British overseas colonies.

When the Broadmead development was still on the drawing board, the Rev. R. W. Waddelow convinced city planners that there was a need to house his congregation above the new shops, with the result that Broadmead Baptist Church was allowed to remain while other city-centre churches moved elsewhere across Bristol. One of Waddelow's successors, the Rev. J. Penry Davies, was closely involved with the development of the new building, envisaging a 'Baptist cathedral of the West'. In recent years, worshippers were instrumental in developing a city-centre Christian chaplaincy that until 2018 served the city's business community, their employees and families. During the week, shoppers and workers can still make use of the church's undercroft, which offers a quiet space in the middle of the hectic day.

Address 1 Whippington Court, Union Street, BS1 3HY, +44 (0)117 929 1387, broadmeadbaptist@gmail.com, www.broadmeadbaptist.org.uk | **Getting there** 3-minute walk from Bristol bus station, entrance next to Tesco Metro | **Hours** Sun worship 11am; Tue lunchtime service 1.10pm | **Tip** Bristol played a major role in the history of chocolate production, with the first mass-produced chocolate bar made in the city by Fry's. The name lives on in Fry's Chocolate Cream, now the world's oldest brand of chocolate. A plaque marks the location of the original Fry factory next to KFC on Union Street.

26 Brunel's Buttery

Banging bacon butties

It may have a Wapping Wharf address, but Brunel's Buttery was here long before the new development nearby opened for business. Coffee can be made a dozen ways in the more expensive cafes nearby. At Brunel's Buttery, it is either black or white. Bovril is also on the menu; this is one of the very few Bristol cafes where it still is. The small cafe occupies a prime harbourside spot a short walk from the SS *Great Britain*, designed by the famous engineer who gives the business its name. Picnic tables outside are prime real estate at busy times, which is often, especially at weekends when a walk along the docks and a bacon sandwich is a magic hangover cure. From the small hatch, combinations of bacon, sausage, egg, cheese and tomato can be ordered, as well as cold sandwiches, pies, pasties, jacket potatoes and cakes. Rock cakes are a particular favourite. Take a ticket and listen out for your number.

Brunel's Buttery was owned and run by Colin and Joan Nutt for over 30 years, until they retired in 2012, a couple of years after an arsonist's fire gutted the kitchen and destroyed its contents. A water heater exploding fortunately kept the whole building from being destroyed. Current owners Gary and Noemi Hands relocated from Cornwall to take up the reins of the business.

In 2018 a statue of Wallace dressed as Ziggy Stardust drinking a mug of tea was unveiled outside the Buttery, marking the new Gromit Unleashed 2 sculpture trail, where more than 60 figures were on display across Bristol raising money for the Children's Hospital. A few years earlier, a local website's April Fool was a story about the cafe turning into a Costa, following the national chain opening on Whiteladies Road and Gloucester Road without the correct planning permission. With the building Photoshopped to look like it had already become part of the national chain, readers reacted with shock and outrage… until they realised the date.

Address Wapping Wharf, BS1 6UD, +44 (0)117 929 1696 | Getting there By boat (either
Bristol Ferry or No. 7) to Wapping Wharf, m2 metrobus to Cumberland Road, or 2-minute
walk from Wapping Wharf | Hours Mon–Fri 8am–4pm, Sat & Sun 8am–5pm | Tip
Take a steam train ride on Bristol Harbour Railway from M Shed pulled by a Bristol-built
steam locomotive, either *Henbury* or *Portbury*, which served their working lives on the docks
railway system at Avonmouth (www.bristolmuseums.org.uk/m-shed).

27 Brunel's Other Bridge

An abandoned piece of engineering history

Bristol's one world-famous landmark is the Clifton Suspension Bridge. Few people know that Isambard Kingdom Brunel also designed an earlier bridge. Hidden under the roads criss-crossing over the Cumberland Basin, Brunel's Other Bridge was the world's first swivel bridge. It may be Grade II*-listed, but it's also on English Heritage's Buildings at Risk Register, and despite the keen volunteers looking after its upkeep, it looks unlikely to swing again. The latest estimated cost of returning it back to everyday use is £700,000.

It is sad to see the bridge in its neglected state, especially compared with photos of its prime, when it formed a key part of the original Cumberland Basin infrastructure, a lot of which was made redundant by the transport system built in the 1960s. The Cumberland Basin is where boats heading into Bristol from the River Avon first arrive. Its locks bring them into the Floating Harbour, which unlike the tidal river remains at a constant height.

The wrought-iron bridge was opened in 1849, 15 years before the Suspension Bridge, to carry traffic over the basin's new south entrance lock. In 1873 it was shortened and relocated to its present position over the north entrance lock, known as Howard's Lock. It rotated on four fixed wheels in contact with a solid ring underneath, originally by a hand crank, later converted to a hydraulic mechanism that ran on pressurised fresh water from nearby Underfall Yard. Brunel can't take full credit for the bridge, but was closely involved in both its design at his Westminster office and its construction at the Great Western Dry Dock, just a few years after the construction of the SS *Great Britain* (where the 'Being Brunel' exhibition is highly recommended). Brunel buffs will be pleased to learn that the bridge represents an early iteration of the flanged-plate girders characterising his later medium-span bridges.

Address Cumberland Basin, Hotwells, BS1 6XS, www.brunelsotherbridge.org.uk | Getting there Walk from the south side of the Cumberland Basin from the m2 metrobus stop near Ashton Avenue Bridge, or from the north side from the bus stop at Merchants Road served by a number of buses | Hours Unrestricted | Tip For the best view of the Clifton Suspension Bridge, cross over the footbridge near Brunel's Other Bridge in the direction of the Create Centre and then immediately turn right taking the footpath down a small slope. Follow this around to an unrivalled vista.

28 Business As Usual

The unofficial home of Bristol cycling

There is something inherently compatible about coffee and cycling. They belong together like Laurel and Hardy, Fred Astaire and Ginger Rogers, and Torville and Dean. Inside speciality coffee shop Full Court Press on Broad Street in the Old City, there is a bicycle pump, and outside there is often a collection of cyclists refuelling after a ride. How else are they able to get up Bristol's multitude of hills without a little caffeine stimulation?

Fortunately, Business As Usual, the unofficial home of Bristol cycling, is a flat ride away from the city centre and conveniently located just a short detour off the Bristol & Bath Railway Path (see ch. 16). It's a collective of three independent companies which joined forces to open in 2018 within a former industrial unit now acting as workshops, retail space, cafe and a social hub. Enjoy a coffee from Camber while you get a bicycle made by Forever Pedalling and then sprayed by Colourburn Studio with a bespoke design. In their own words, 'under one roof, a world class mechanic, the most talented painter in the industry and delicious coffee'.

Most of the walls here may be painted white, but there is a riot of colour from dozens of cycling caps hanging both for display and for sale, and tubes painted by former Dyson model-maker Rob Nicholas of Colourburn – including samples made for the bikes Connor Swift won the British national road championships on in 2018 and 2019.

Tim Wilkey's Forever Pedalling workshop is usually a hive of activity, especially when a ride from the Das Rad Klub cycling club that he founded starts from Business As Usual, or when fans crowd around the televisions to watch one of the grand tours. Too much caffeine in your system after your expertly made coffee from Andy Matthews' Camber cafe? Better visit the loo, which has a sign on the door saying *contrôle antidopage*. Chapeau!

Address Unit 3, Russell Town Avenue, Lawrence Hill, BS5 9LT, businessasusualcc@gmail.com, www.businessasusual.cc | **Getting there** 1-minute walk from Lawrence Hill train station, where several buses also stop; by bike, leave the Bristol & Bath Railway Path at Russell Town Avenue. Walk through blue gates to right of Door World towards the back of the yard, through the roller shutter door on left. | **Hours** Wed–Fri 8am–6pm, Sat 9am–5pm, Sun 10am–5pm | **Tip** Follow the smell of freshly baked bread to Church Road in Redfield to find The Bristol Loaf. Watch the dedicated team at work in the open-plan bakery while enjoying their breads, savouries, pastries and cakes, as well as coffee and soft drinks (www.thebristolloaf.co.uk).

29 — Cafe Wall Illusion

An accidental trick of the eye

If you Google 'optical illusion', among images of an elephant that appears to have eight legs, and two faces with a vase in between them, is a series of what at first seem to be wonky horizontal lines separated by a series of dark and white squares. Look more closely, however, and the lines are not wonky at all but perfectly parallel. The specific pattern of the squares has led to your eyes tricking your brain.

The official name of this particular illusion is the 'cafe wall illusion' and it has its origins in an unusual tiling pattern outside a cafe whose position close to the University of Bristol led inadvertently to its fame in the field of brain-bamboozlement. The illusion was first reported in 1979 by Richard Gregory, a professor of neuropsychology, after Steve Simpson, a member of his laboratory team, observed the unusual visual effect of the chessboard-like design.

The boffins discovered that cortex confusion is caused when offset dark and light tiles are alternated, creating the illusion of tapering horizontal lines – with the effect depending on the presence of a line of grey mortar between the tiles. The science behind the illusion, written by Gregory with Priscilla Heard, was first published in the scholarly journal *Perception*, in which they wrote about the 'inappropriate contour shifts from neighbouring regions of contrasting luminance'.

The illusion is located outside a cafe now called 404 Not Found, which for many years was a butcher's. In a previous incarnation, the space also housed Special K's, a popular hangout of the Wild Bunch collective who would later spawn Massive Attack, the biggest band to ever emerge from Bristol. Special K's was close to both the flat of Grant Marshall on the bottom of St Michael's Hill, and legendary former nightclub The Dug Out on Park Row, where Marshall (also known as Daddy G) and his fellow Wild Bunch members made their name in the 1980s at what was then the epicentre of Bristol's music scene.

Address 404 Not Found, 19-20 Perry Road, BS1 5BG, www.404bristol.com | Getting there Always accessible | Hours 3-minute walk from the Wills Memorial Building | Tip Cross the road to find the charming Christmas Steps. Known as Knyfesmith Street in medieval times, its current name could be a reference to a stained-glass nativity scene in the Three Kings of Cologne Chapel at the top of the steps. Buy a special bottle in Weber & Tring's or get your bassoon repaired by Trevor Jones (www.christmasstepsartsquarter.co.uk).

30 Campus Pool Skatepark
Where skating has replaced splashing

This purpose-built, indoor, concrete skatepark is inside a disused swimming pool in Bishopsworth, one of the most southerly bits of Bristol before you hit the countryside. Campus' two founders, a youth worker and a social worker, set out to use skateboarding as a tool to engage with children and young people, opening this space in July 2015. An on-site cafe, The Daily Grind (geddit?), hosts numerous community events and serves a good cup of coffee and slice of cake. It also acts as a crèche for parents on their phones or reading a book while waiting while their children enjoy a skate or a scoot. The kids occasionally pop into the cafe for a glass of water or can from the fridge before speeding off again.

Once a village within the Somerset parish of Bedminster, Bishopsworth was only absorbed into the confines of the city of Bristol in 1951. Campus Pool is now located where a small chapel dedicated to St Peter and St Paul was built in the late 12th century. An agreement provided for a chaplain to visit from Bedminster three times a week, which continued for several centuries until the chapel was converted into three cottages. These stood until the city council demolished them in 1961 to make way for the swimming pool, now Bristol's most unusual skatepark.

The Pool's sister venue is the Park, a wooden build within a former youth centre in Winterbourne, to the north of Bristol. The Pool retains many of the features of the old swimming pool it was until the 1970s, making for a quirky and original space. Among the concrete ramps are tiles that swimmers used to push off from, which are now jumped over using a great variety of tricks. They can be glimpsed behind glass from a viewing gallery that doubles up as a shop. Sessions here include 'toddler takeovers' for children five and under, skateboard-only and girls-only sessions, as well as classes for newbies.

Address Whitchurch Road, Bishopsworth, BS13 7RW, +44 (0)117 964 1478, info@campusskateparks.co.uk, www.campusskateparks.co.uk | Getting there Cycle with your skateboard on your back along the Malago Greenway, or bus 75 to Church Road | Hours Daily 10am–9pm (check website for specific sessions) | Tip Bishopsworth's most historic building, Bishopsworth Manor on Church Road, was built around 1720 in a similar style to the much larger Kings Weston House. It is now a Grade II*-listed private residence.

31 Castle Park Pyramid

Going underground

A small concrete pyramid marks the entrance to a vaulted cellar that once stood underneath the heart of the medieval city. It is one of a multitude of chambers that date back to the 12th century, with this part of Bristol said to have been honeycombed with similar spaces. Many were interlinked, with some historians believing that it was possible to walk underground from Corn Street all the way to the area now covered by Castle Park, Bristol's bustling commercial centre, until it was almost completely annihilated by German bombs during World War II. Despite the above-ground destruction, these medieval cellars were built to last, with some surviving direct hits during Luftwaffe raids.

In her book, *Secret Underground Bristol*, Sally Watson, who studied archaeology at the University of Bristol, calls what is accessed down a rickety spiral staircase via a locked door on one side of the pyramid 'some of the finest medieval cellars in Britain, with beautiful rib-vaulted ceilings which would not disgrace a Gothic cathedral'. One example of ancient underground cellars still in use are those owned by Averys wine merchants (see ch. 6) close to the foot of Park Street; other cellars around King Street and also Small Street are now in use as restaurants or nightclubs.

It is difficult to imagine now but close to the pyramid, at the corner of Wine Street and High Street, stood the Dutch House, a well-known local landmark with a five-storey timber frame. It was once a private residence, then a bank, and following that several different retail and office spaces. Its last occupier before the war was the Irish Linen & Hosiery Association. Over the years there has been regular talk of bringing this somewhat neglected corner of Bristol back to life, with more ambitious plans including the rebuilding of the Dutch House. Perhaps we will one day again have access to Bristol's underground history. Watch this space.

Address High Street, BS1 2AW (almost opposite junction with St Nicholas Street) | Getting there 1-minute walk from St Nick's Market | Hours Pyramid always accessible, but no public access to cellars | Tip St Nicholas Market – known to most people simply as St Nick's – is a collection of unique independent stalls within what was originally Bristol's corn exchange. Look out for regular night markets, when the stalls spill out onto the surrounding streets (www.stnicholasmarketbristol.co.uk).

32 Chance & Counters

Fancy a game?

At the last count, there were almost 900 games to play at Bristol's original board-game cafe, with one of the punniest names in the city. The sounds of dice being rolled, tiles shaken or cards shuffled are the background noises here, with colour-coded game boxes taking up one entire wall. If you get stuck, knowledgeable staff will be able to help you with even the most complicated instruction manual; if you are on your own, Monday evening is the time to visit, when players can be matched up with like-minded gamers; and if you need sustenance, there is a food menu featuring the likes of wraps and sandwiches, and a large drinks selection including chocolate bar-themed milkshakes and a good variety of locally brewed beers.

Chance & Counters was founded by three friends in 2016 following a successful crowdfunding campaign. Customers pay for their table by the hour, and such is the draw of some of the games that an entire rainy day (or a four-hour maximum at the busiest times) can easily be taken up on a tropical island with the threat of an imminent tsunami or helping a rhinoceros climb up a growing tower of cards.

Since opening in Bristol, two other Chance & Counters have also opened in Cardiff and Birmingham, and immersive gaming events have been held in venues including the Good Chemistry brewery in St Phillip's.

On a recent visit to the cafe, a member of staff recommended a game called Tsuro to two new visitors. They were soon laying tiles in front of their token to continue its path along a board that had been used so many times it had split into quarters. If you feel like being a guinea pig, you can play brand new games conceived and created by local games designers on the first Tuesday of every month, on play-testing night. 'One more game?' goes the familiar refrain from friends on one table. There are plenty to choose from.

Address 20 Christmas Steps, BS1 5BS, +44 (0)117 329 1700, theteam@chanceandcounters.com, www.chanceandcounters.com/bristol | **Getting there** Sun–Wed 10am–11pm, Thu–Sat 10am–midnight | **Hours** Bottom of Christmas Steps, 5-minute walk from Cascade Steps | **Tip** Walk up Christmas Steps and turn right on Colston Street to find Bloom & Curll bookshop. If he is not bookbinding in the back room, owner Jason Beech may be out among the wonderful array of new and second-hand books. No stockroom means all the books for sale are on display (www.bloomandcurll.co.uk).

33 Charles Wesley's House

A home of hymns

Even if you haven't heard of Charles Wesley, you might very well have sung some of his hymns. The co-founder of the Methodist movement in the Church of England is known as the 'father of the English hymn' and it is reckoned that he wrote more than 9,000 during his lifetime. Among the most famous are 'Love Divine, All Loves Excelling' and that Christmas classic, 'Hark, the Herald Angels Sing'.

From 1749 to 1771, Charles lived in Bristol with his wife, Sally, and their children. This house on Charles Street (a road which only coincidentally shares his name) was the family's last Bristol home before they moved to London, and it was the place where Charles wrote many of his best-known hymns. It is a remarkable survivor of its time, from when the road was described as 'not a highly desirable residential location'. Today it is situated between modern office buildings and student flats, with only a small plaque giving an indication of its history. The house itself shows visitors what an 18th-century family home might have looked like, as well as information about Charles' work.

Like the more well-known Georgian House museum, Charles Wesley's House has been decorated in period fixtures and fittings to be as authentic as possible to its era. Among the rooms are the music room with a harpsichord that is still used in concerts; Charles' study recreated under the rafters of the roof, with a very rare surviving example of a Georgian attic fire; and a kitchen in the basement, where the Wesleys' servants would have heated water to take to various other parts of the house, and where they cooked the family's breakfast favourites of broth and porridge. Two hundred years after the departure of the Wesleys, breakfast was still being served in the house, which from the 1930s to the 1990s was used as accommodation for Methodist students.

Address 4 Charles Street, BS1 3NN, info@newroombristol.org.uk, www.charleswesleyhouse.org.uk | Getting there 2-minute walk from Bristol bus station | Hours Open for pre-booked groups of ten people or more | Tip Bristol's best music shop is located a stone's throw away on Stokes Croft. Originally specialising in pianos, Mickleburgh is a proudly independent retailer, and one of the biggest music shops in the UK (www.mickleburgh.co.uk).

34 Chatterton's Cafe
Paninis and poetry

Dating from 1749, the former home of boy poet Thomas Chatterton is incongruously marooned on a small patch of grass located between the thundering traffic of Redcliffe Way and the cobbles of Portwall Lane. Empty for more than a decade after closing as a museum dedicated to Chatterton's life, the council-owned building was given a new lease of life when it reopened as Chatterton's Cafe in 2016. The unfussy food here is of the panini, jacket potato and pasty variety, with full English breakfasts served from 7am aiming to tempt the early morning commuters en route to nearby Temple Meads railway station, and free refills of filter coffee. The house is opposite 800-year-old St Mary Redcliffe Church, where the office of sexton had long been held by a member of Chatterton's family – a connection which allowed him access to its ancient treasures.

It's a rare joy to see such an important Bristol building brought back to life. But far more interesting than its typical cafe fare is Chatterton, whose extraordinary life was due to be celebrated in 2020 in a series of events as part of 'A Poetic City' to mark the 250th anniversary of his death. Born in Bristol in 1752, the precocious child began writing poetry around the age of 10. He wrote both under his own name and also took part in an elaborate deception, claiming to have found the lost works of a 15th-century Bristol monk, Thomas Rowley, devoting himself to writing as the fictitious character and in the process becoming an early pioneer of the Romantic genre. He left Bristol for London in the hope of finding his fortune. A comic opera brought in some money but he struggled financially, refusing the offer of food from friends, and died impoverished in 1770 aged just 17 after taking arsenic. The unhappy Romantic enjoyed little attention in his short life, but found great posthumous fame, influencing the likes of William Wordsworth and John Keats.

Address Redcliffe Way, BS1 6NA | **Getting there** 3-minute walk from Bristol Temple Meads | **Hours** Mon–Fri 7am–3pm | **Tip** There is a bronze statue of Chatterton on Millennium Square, alongside others of William Penn, founder of the US state of Pennsylvania; William Tyndale, who translated the Bible into English; and Archibald Leach, who found fame in Hollywood as actor Cary Grant.

35 _ Cheers Drive

Bristol's very own Boaty McBoatface

Catch a bus anywhere in Bristol and you will hear passengers say, 'Cheers, drive', when they get off at their stop (except if you are on a metrobus route because those buses have their exit doors in the middle of the vehicle, but that's another story). 'Cheers, drive' in Bristolian vernacular is the standard way of kindly thanking your bus driver. And in 2020 a new road was given the name of Cheers Drive following a poll of local residents: the city's very own Boaty McBoatface.

Cheers Drive is part of the new Whitewood Park development of homes off Brook Road in Speedwell. The other new roads in the development, on land that previously contained warehouses, are Ron Stone Road, named after a former councillor; Dening Gardens, named after Charles Dening, the architect of Speedwell Pool; and Kenney Lane, named after Annie Kenney, a militant suffragette. Developers Persimmon Homes unusually asked the city council to help name the new roads. Local councillor Mhairi Threlfall was given the task and she decided to put it out to a public poll – with the theme of Bristol – to Speedwell and Eastville residents. 'Cheers Drive was suggested and came top so I submitted it,' Threlfall told *Bristol24/7*. 'That was back in May 2018 so it's been cracking me up for about two years! All thanks to a public poll, the creative people of Speedwell and the great people at Persimmon Homes!'

Cheers Drive might be the new kid on the block, but it's not the only road name in Bristol to raise a smile. The bins behind the Bristol & Bath Rum Distillery on Park Street are the lucky permanent residents of There and Back Again Lane; just in case Saffron Close, Sage Hill and Rosemary Lane do not accurately portray our love of food, we also have Cheese Lane and Ham Lane; and Nowhere Lane in Nailsea is the road for you if you want to reside somewhere inconspicuous.

Address Cheers Drive, Speedwell, BS5 7FQ | Getting there 5-minute cycle from the Bristol & Bath Railway Path, or bus 6 to Brook Road | Hours Unrestricted | Tip To say 'cheers, drive' to an imaginary bus driver, climb aboard the double-decker bus on the ground floor of the M Shed museum. Previously in service across Bristol, this Lodekka bus was built in 1966 and withdrawn from use in 1983 (www.bristolmuseums.org.uk/m-shed).

36 Cider at the Orchard

Enjoy some West Country champagne

Being the biggest city in the West Country and known as the smallest big city in the UK, Bristol is surrounded by the rolling fields of Somerset and Gloucestershire. These are conveniently home to some of the UK's best cider producers, but, paradoxically, these days it is far easier to get good beer in Bristol than good cider. Don't tell that to the regulars at The Orchard Inn, though. This free house has been selling cider on the premises since 1834 and today always stocks more than 20 still ciders and perries from across the West Country and Wales, with names like Janet's Jungle Juice, Slack-Ma-Girdle and Haymaker. There is beer, wine and spirits as well, but it is really all about the cider here, which can be accompanied by fresh rolls, and, if you're lucky, a blues or piano jam.

Steph Iles and Sam Marriott had a tough act to follow when they took over the running of the Orchard in 2018, as in recent years it had won numerous awards, including the Campaign for Real Ale's national cider pub of the year in 2009, as well as numerous regional accolades. But they quickly added to the awards cabinet with the Crumbs Award for Bristol's best pub in 2019.

During the coronavirus pandemic the following year, they kept their locals watered even when the pub was shut by selling takeaway cider flagons.

Want some local cider to take home? Head to Bristol Cider Shop's online store. Originally based on Christmas Steps and later in Wapping Wharf, they now only trade online but still host regular tasting events. Visit the Apple, a cider bar on a boat moored off Welsh Back, for a drink inside in the winter and outside in the summer. And in Clifton, it has long been a tradition for students to go to the Coronation Tap to get 'Corried' – a colloquial term for enjoying some of their strongest ciders (although the new landlords disapprove of this practice).

Address The Orchard Inn, Hanover Place, Spike Island, BS1 6XT, +44 (0)7405 360994, theorchardinnpub@gmail.com, www.orchardinn.co.uk | Getting there 2-minute walk from SS *Great Britain*; metrobus m2 to Cumberland Road | Hours Mon–Fri noon–11pm, Sat & Sun 11am–11pm | Tip Just around the corner from the Orchard is Spike Island, home to gallery space, artists' studios and the excellent Emmeline cafe (www.spikeisland.org.uk).

37 __ Circomedia
Run away to join the circus

There is always something extraordinary happening in Circomedia, Bristol's globally renowned centre of circus and physical theatre. Its headquarters are in a former church in St Paul's, with a satellite site within a former school in Kingswood. From five-year-olds at an after-school class making their first tentative steps across a tightrope to adults defying gravity on the flying trapeze high above audiences' heads, Circomedia appeals as much to young adventure-seekers as to people who really have run away to join the circus. Keep an eye on their calendar to book tickets for spellbinding shows from both visiting international companies and current students, or if you're feeling the call of the big top yourself, sign up for classes in everything from juggling to handstands.

Circomedia began life in 1994 as the descendent of Fool Time, the UK's first full-time circus school. In 2017, it launched the world's first postgraduate master's degree in directing circus. The following year, plans were revealed to develop a purpose-built facility at the Bottle Yard Studios (see ch. 14) in Hengrove, which if it goes ahead would become the largest centre for circus in the UK, with state-of-the-art facilities for more than 130 full-time students to study and train.

'Here at Circomedia, we are dedicated to creating a limitless space where people can discover the fullness of their physical, emotional and creative potential,' say the team. 'We aim to be the UK's centre for research and production of transformational experiences arising from circus.' They do this through offering full-time education at post-16, undergraduate and postgraduate levels; through their eclectic performance programme featuring companies that push the boundaries of circus and physical theatre; through their classes that inspire people of all ages to discover circus skills; and through working within the community to promote 'the liberating possibilities' of this extraordinary artform.

Address St Paul's Church, Portland Square, St Paul's, BS2 8SJ, +44 (0)117 924 7615, info@circomedia.com, www.circomedia.com | **Getting there** 3-minute walk from Cabot Circus; close to multiple buses that stop on Bond Street or City Road | **Hours** Mon–Fri 9am–4pm (box office and general enquiries) | **Tip** The UK's fifth Artist Residence hotel was due to open in 2020 in a former boot factory on one corner of Portland Square following three years of restoration work. The 23-bedroom hotel promises to be a new 'neighbourhood hangout' with coffee shop, bar, kitchen, event space and garden (www.artistresidence.co.uk/bristol).

38 Clifton Rocks Railway

A fun and fascinating funicular

The Portway is a main artery into Bristol, and is usually choked with traffic. When the road was first built alongside the River Avon through the Avon Gorge, however, it offered a picturesque location for a quiet promenade. It was even featured in illustrations promoting the joys of Bristol to tourists.

As the crow flies, Clifton may be close to the river and the large wooden jetties that used to welcome pleasure steamers, but its topography, high above the Portway with steep cliffs in between, proved prohibitive. So how best to connect wealthy Cliftonites to these opportunities down below, without spoiling the world-famous view of the gorge and Suspension Bridge spanning its width? Easy. Build a railway through the rocks from top to bottom. First proposed in 1880, work began in 1891 and lasted for two years, with a 500-foot-long brick-lined tunnel blasted and cut through limestone, climbing a vertical distance of 240 feet. At the time of construction, the tunnel was the widest of its kind in the world, with two cars on adjacent tracks powered by hydraulic pressure. Almost half a million passengers in the first 12 months proved to be its peak as a funicular railway. The widening of the Portway in 1922 placed the major road mere inches from the bottom station, and after a steady decline the last cars ran in 1934.

But that wasn't the end of its story. During World War II, Bristolians occupied the tunnels to shelter from German bombing, before the BBC built studios inside so they could continue broadcasting. For many years, volunteers have looked after the railway, tidying, painting and acting as tour guides. In 2019, the site was purchased by Ian Johnson, a businessman who also owns the nearby Clifton Observatory, whose plans are to open a museum at the upper station seven days a week and gradually restore the historic railway to its original Victorian glory.

Address Sion Hill, Clifton, BS8 4LD, www.cliftonrocksrailway.org.uk | **Getting there** 2-minute walk from Clifton Suspension Bridge; 3-minute walk from bus 8 stop on Clifton Down Road | **Hours** Open to the public during occasional open days | **Tip** Clifton Suspension Bridge is undoubtedly Bristol's most famous landmark. Designed by Isambard Kingdom Brunel and opened in 1864, it is still yielding surprises such as the vaulted chambers within the Leigh Woods tower that were only rediscovered in 2002 (www.cliftonbridge.org.uk).

39___ Clifton Rock Slide

Polished smooth by generations of bottoms

In 2014, Bristol artist Luke Jerram installed a giant water slide down Park Street. Running for one day only, almost 100,000 people signed up for their chance to get a 'ticket to slide' through an online ballot. Jerram's slide has since been recreated in other cities across the world but even though it was a one-off, only a mile and a half away there is a slide open all year round. Unofficially the sign that you have become a bona fide Bristol native if you have slid your way down to the bottom, the Clifton rock slide is a natural rock formation close to the Clifton Suspension Bridge that has been rubbed smooth and shiny by thousands of sliding posteriors over many years.

It actually doesn't have an official name. Clifton rock slide seems its most suitable moniker for our purposes, but it is also known as the slidey rock, the sliding rock, the slippery rocks or just the slider – the latter thanks to the local vernacular (see also, to 'smooth' rather than pet a dog, and the obligatory 'cheers, drive' (see ch. 35) when getting off the bus). The slide is easy to spot, with the natural rock formation next to a footpath perfectly suited for some fun on your way to see the picture-postcard view of the bridge. Once you have found it, you need to hop over a fence, get your bottom into position and then let gravity do the rest. Make sure you have your wits about you, as depending on what clothes you are wearing on your lower half, you can quickly build up speed during your descent.

The origins of the rock slide are lost in the mists of time. But it is fascinating to think that perhaps even fun-loving Iron Age tribespeople might too have slid down here, with one of Bristol's three ancient hill forts situated just a few hundred yards away on what is now Observatory Hill, with two others on the other side of the Avon Gorge possibly once occupied by different groups from the same Dobunni tribe.

Address Litfield Road, Clifton, BS8 3LT | **Getting there** Less than a minute's walk from Clifton Suspension Bridge, accessed off footpath heading up towards Clifton Observatory from Suspension Bridge Road | **Hours** Unrestricted | **Tip** Originally built as a windmill in 1766, the Clifton Observatory now contains one of only three camera obscuras in the UK, is the access point for the Giant's Cave and is the home of a cafe with a terrace offering unrivalled views of the Clifton Suspension Bridge (www.cliftonobservatory.com).

40__Convoy Espresso

Cracking coffee in converted caravans

When the first sketch was made of the proposed transformation of a former paint factory hugging the River Avon in south Bristol into space for new offices and homes, a converted Airstream caravan was included in the design. Fast-forward two decades and two converted Airstream caravans now sit within the Paintworks development, surrounded by Victorian brick buildings housing tech companies, photography studios and trendy New York-style loft apartments.

If you head out of Bristol on Bath Road past Temple Meads, look out for a spaceship rotating around a yellow planet the size of a small boulder. This still says Tube Diner, a reminder of what used to be a traditional greasy spoon. It was completely ripped out by three friends – a photographer, a web developer and a teacher – to become Convoy Espresso in 2018. Initially, there was some consternation from locals that there would no longer be any artery-blocking bacon butties. But Convoy has steadily built up its regular customers who come for expertly made coffee, pastries from Assembly Bakery and beer from Tapestry just the other side of the river. Cookies are kept in one glass jar on the counter, with another glass jar the perfect shape for Dutch stroopwafels to melt on top of your morning brew.

Half of one of the silver bullet-shaped caravans is the kitchen where drinks are made and toasties freshly prepared every day by Ri and her team. The other caravan is just for seating, with foliage cascading down the walls. Internationally renowned Magnum photographer Martin Parr has his Foundation in the Paintworks, and in 2019 he used the inside of this caravan for a photo shoot. If it looks good enough for him, it looks good enough for us. Just remember to bring your plastic, because like many new food and drink businesses opening in Bristol these days, Convoy Espresso does not accept cash.

Address Paintworks, Bath Road, Arnos Vale, BS4 3EH, hello@convoyespresso.com, www.convoyespresso.com | **Getting there** 10-minute walk from Bristol Temple Meads; bus 1, 39, 178 to Bath Road | **Hours** Mon–Fri 7.45am–4.45pm | **Tip** If just enjoying a coffee in a converted Airstream caravan is not good enough for you, you can stay the night in one at Brooks Guesthouse, which has three silver caravans perched on their roof on AstroTurf lawns overlooking St Nick's Market (www.brooksguesthousebristol.com).

41 Cross-harbour Ferry

A fun way to get from A to B

Bristol is a city built around water, with the Floating Harbour once a thriving centre of industry. Do you know the phrase, 'shipshape and Bristol fashion'? It's from the days when ships entering Bristol's docks had to make sure their cargo was carefully secured so it didn't fall off as the tides rose high and fell very low.

The tidal range of the River Avon is the second greatest of any in the world, with the water level in Bristol changing as much as 12 metres. Eighteenth-century merchants employed engineers, who later included Isambard Kingdom Brunel, to make the harbour non-tidal by damming the river. Construction was completed in 1809, allowing ships in the harbour to stay afloat, hence a 'Floating Harbour'. In Brunel's day, several ferry services allowed dock workers to easily cross the water. The name of Gaol Ferry Bridge, connecting Wapping Wharf to Southville, is a reminder of this, with neither the gaol nor the ferry remaining. Now, just one cross-harbour service plies from one side to the other. Run by Number Seven Boat Trips, it costs £1.20 for adults to cross from the Harbour Inlet (also known as Brunel Quay, where you can enjoy food and drink at Broken Dock and Spoke & Stringer) to the SS *Great Britain*, with the journey taking only around a minute. The boat, named *Mary Brunel* after Brunel's daughter, is a Rotork Seatruck, originally co-designed for military use by James Dyson of vacuum-cleaner fame while he was still a student at the Royal College of Art.

On weekdays, join commuters heading from south of the river to work in the city centre and back again on what is undoubtedly Bristol's most picturesque and serene commute. While onboard, don't mind having to squeeze up tight while sitting next to your fellow passengers, and admire the skill of the pilots as they manoeuvre to the two docking stations with the subtlest of movements of the propeller.

Address From Harbour Inlet to SS *Great Britain* | Getting there Metrobus m2 and Bristol Insight guided tour bus stop on Cumberland Road close to SS *Great Britain*; Harbour Inlet is 3-minute walk from Millennium Square | Hours Daily except Dec 25 and 26, Mon–Fri 7.30am–6.15pm, Sat & Sun 10.30am–5.30pm | Tip If you prefer navigating the Floating Harbour under your own steam, book a stand-up paddleboarding session with SUP Bristol (www.supbristol.com).

42__The Cube

Much more than just a cinema

The history of the building which is home to the Cube Microplex is almost as eclectic as what happens now within its four walls. It has previously been a glass recycling depot, an amateur-dramatics theatre, a gay avant-garde art centre, an extension of the Chinese Overseas Association, a girls' school, a deaf and dumb institute, a secret gig venue, and an illegal gambling den. Today, the Cube is run by a dedicated group of volunteers as a not-for-profit workers' cooperative, screening films, putting on live music, making their own-recipe cola and much more. Anybody can attend as long as they are a member – which costs just £1 for life.

The Cube was formed in 1998 by four artists who freely admit they had no idea what they were getting into. The am-dram group had built the wooden staging themselves, with this DIY ethic living on in the volunteers who are the lifeblood of the building.

'We are amateurs, but we resist the negative connotations of that word,' they say. Some of Bristol's most memorable evenings of entertainment take place in this higgledy-piggledy building in a sort of no-man's-land between Stokes Croft, Kingsdown and the city centre.

Whether it be cinema or live music, cabaret or comedy, the Cube's programme is not easily definable. Regular events include morning film screenings for parents and carers with babies under one, a house orchestra, and a short film version of open-mic nights. They have sent volunteers to Haiti to screen films for earthquake survivors, provide an internet server for Kingsdown, pride themselves on being Bristol's cheapest cinema and give free entry to all of their events to asylum seekers. In 2014, following an extraordinary outpouring of generosity from the Bristol public, the Cube team raised £185,000 in order to buy the building, and have since carried on as eclectically as ever.

Address Dove Street South, Kingsdown, BS2 8JD, +44 (0)117 907 4190, cubeadmin@cubecinema.com, www.cubecinema.com | Getting there 5-minute walk from either Bristol bus station or Stokes Croft | Hours Usually daily, but check listings for film and event times | Tip You would hope that the films at the Cube are only good ones. If you want a guaranteed stinker, however, look no further than Bristol Bad Film Club, who revel in screening so-bad-they're-great cult classics (www.bristolbadfilmclub.co.uk).

43__Cumberland Piazza

Under-flyover art

The largest open space in Hotwells once complemented a road scheme which callously cut through a swathe of the area in the 1960s. Distinguished landscape architect, Dame Sylvia Crow, was responsible for the Cumberland Piazza, in which she put water fountains, trees and a playground with a 'nautical flavour'. It enjoyed a brief heyday, but growth in traffic meant neglect, and the space was effectively abandoned until recent years. Locals led by Ray Smith and later Anna Haydock-Wilson have now brought back some life, including murals painted by children from the nearby Hotwells Primary School in collaboration with artist Amy Hutchings, and splashes of colour added to the columns supporting the elevated roads.

It was all once so different. From the 1760s, elegant terraces, gardens and an assembly room were built up around the development of the Hotwells spa. The spa's decline in the early 19th century coincided with the development of Bristol as a port, with the Cumberland Basin a central element of the Floating Harbour. Grand houses were replaced by commercial buildings and tenements for industrial workers. In 1963, the whole area on which the piazza now stands – including the assembly room, three streets and five pubs – was demolished to make way for a new road system. The original piazza plans are now largely forgotten, with circular formations of bricks all that remains of fountains, pools and play areas.

If the Cumberland Piazza is a remnant of over-ambitious 1960s' planning, what could come next here is just as bold. Under proposals for the so-called 'Western Harbour' development first revealed in 2019 by Bristol mayor Marvin Rees, most of the elevated road system and the Plimsoll swing bridge will be demolished to make way for thousands of new dwellings built in response to the city's housing crisis. Homes could soon be returning to this corner of Hotwells.

Address Hotwell Road, Hotwells, BS8 4UB, www.hotwellscliftonwood.org.uk | Getting there Steep 5-minute walk down Granby Hill from Royal York Crescent, or walk along the Floating Harbour from the city centre; bus to Christina Terrace; ferry to the Pump House | Hours Unrestricted | Tip On the other side of the docks from the Cumberland Piazza is Lockside, a restaurant underneath one of the elevated roads which found fame as Sid's Cafe in *Only Fools & Horses* (www.lockside.net).

44_ Dowry Square
Find yourself in hot water

The grand squares and crescents of Clifton may get most of the attention these days, but it was Hotwells that first attracted the great and good of Georgian society due to the quality of its spa waters, once rivalling Bath. Laid out from 1721 as one of the first significant developments associated with the spa, Dowry Square is one of the few remaining examples of Hotwells' heyday, while much of this corner of Bristol was demolished to make way for a new road network (see ch. 43). It hasn't been just spa waters here either; German watchmaker Jacob Schweppe began selling his carbonated water from a shop on the square in 1812.

Look up to the roof level above what is now number 13 and you'll see 'Clifton Dispensary'. The UK is now exceptionally fortunate to have its National Health Service (NHS) providing free healthcare to all, but prior to its foundation in 1948, falling sick could be a costly business. Dispensaries were created mostly in the 19th century as an alternative to hospitals or doctors, whose remedies often made things worse. They provided medical care mostly for the poor, with Thomas Beddoes' Dispensary (later incorporated into the Clifton Dispensary) founded on Dowry Square in 1799.

The fact that Dowry Square today looks much like it did 300 years ago is largely due to the efforts of former resident Peter Ware (1929–1999); a plaque recognises his work. Other plaques dotted around the square commemorate Sir Humphrey Davy (1778–1829), who carried out research into the use of nitrous oxide gas as an anaesthetic and invented the Davy lamp for miners (his assistant Peter Roget went on to publish an eponymous thesaurus); and William Pennington (1740–1829), who was master of ceremonies at the former Hotwells assembly room for 30 years, and no doubt known by all of the movers and shakers in the city's grand Georgian society who took the spa waters.

Address Dowry Square, Hotwells, BS8 4SH | **Getting there** 5-minute walk from Royal York Crescent, or 20-minute walk along the Floating Harbour from the city centre; bus to Christina Terrace; ferry to the Pump House | **Hours** Unrestricted | **Tip** Underfall Yard – the other side of Merchants Road bridge from Dowry Square – remains a working shipyard, with wooden boats being built as they have been here for centuries and a visitor centre telling the story of the Floating Harbour through hands-on displays (www.underfallyard.co.uk).

45 Everard's Printing Works

An Art Nouveau advertisement

Edward Everard's Printing Works is Bristol's own version of Times Square, with an Art Nouveau tiled façade replacing the neon lights of New York City. Set back from its neighbours on historic Broad Street, its riot of colours still springs as much of a surprise on unsuspecting passers-by today as it did when it was built in 1900, when visitors were said to have come to scoff at its gaudiness. First and foremost, it is a brilliant advert for Everard's business, but the frontage also tells the history of printing, with skilled marketer Everard writing himself into the centre of the story.

Everard was a great admirer of William Morris, the founder of the Arts and Crafts movement; Morris is depicted on the right-hand side of the façade.

The spirit of literature is represented in the centre, and on the left side is Johann Gutenberg, the inventor of the printing press that brought printing to Europe. On the gable is a female figure holding a lamp and mirror to symbolise light and truth. Everard's name can be found in an Art Nouveau typeface that he designed himself, above wrought-iron gates incorporating his initials. The decorative ceramic tiles were made by Doulton's and designed by the famous firm's chief artist, William James Neatby, who went on to design the tiles in Harrods' London food hall in 1903. The façade was quite the welcome to Everard's printing business, which once stretched back from Broad Street and behind neighbouring properties to another entrance on John Street.

In 2020, plans were well underway to completely refurbish and extend the vacant 1970s' office block surrounding the former printing works and create shops, bars, restaurants and flats, with the façade due to become the grand entrance of a four-star hotel from Ireland's Dalata Hotel Group. Whatever happens next, Everard's name will live on – a grand advertisement to stand the test of time.

Address 37 Broad Street, BS1 2EQ | Getting there 3-minute walk from St Nick's Market | Hours Unrestricted | Tip Walk down John Street from the Everard's façade to find The Bank Tavern, which in 2019 was named the winner of the UK's best Sunday lunch at The Observer Food Monthly Awards (www.banktavern.com).

46 Elizabeth Blackwell's House

Prejudice-fighting female physician

Despite becoming the first woman to receive a medical degree in the United States and the first woman on the UK Medical Register, medicine was never the overarching calling for Elizabeth Blackwell. Rather, it was the fight for gender equality. Blackwell also campaigned to abolish slavery, for morality in government and for the liberalisation of Victorian prudery. She has been remembered on a US stamp and in a statue at her former medical school in New York. Yet in Bristol, the place of her birth in 1821, a small plaque on her former home in St Paul's is remarkably unremarkable.

Blackwell was certainly not from a privileged background. Her father, Samuel, moved his wife and ten children to America when Elizabeth was 11 years old. When Samuel died only a few years after emigrating, Blackwell and her sisters began teaching to earn money for the family. After a family friend claimed she would have received more considerate treatment from a female doctor, Blackwell became determined to train as a physician. But she was rejected by every single medical school she applied to apart from one, who admitted her as a joke. Two years later, she broke new ground for women with her medical degree. She worked in clinics in Paris and London, and on her return to America in 1851 founded the New York Infirmary for Women & Children, the first hospital for, staffed and run by women.

North Bristol's new £430m Southmead Hospital, opened in 2014, might have been named after Blackwell if the decision hadn't been made to keep its original moniker. Her name still lives on in the University of Bristol's Elizabeth Blackwell Institute for Health Research, which brings together researchers from diverse fields in order to make a real impact on health and healthcare, as well as ensuring that Blackwell's ambitions for equality are continued today.

Address 1 Wilson Street, St Paul's, BS2 9HH | Getting there 2-minute walk from Cabot Circus | Hours Unrestricted view of exterior | Tip Built as a 16th-century party house, the Red Lodge contains the last complete Elizabethan room in Bristol. The lodge became the UK's first girls' reform school in 1854 at a time when the solution used to be the workhouse or prison (www.bristolmuseums.org.uk/red-lodge-museum).

The first
woman doctor

Elizabeth

Blackwell
1821 - 1910

lived here

donated by the
MEDICAL WOMEN'S FEDERATION
and friends

47 __ The Exchange

A music venue owned by music fans

For many years, Bristol's proud musical pedigree was limited in the minds of many people to the narrow genre of trip-hop thanks to the global success of Massive Attack and Portishead. You don't have to dig too far beneath the surface, however, to find new music bubbling away.

On any night of the week, it's possible to enjoy unique live music experiences including the newest bands at the Thekla, jazz at the Old Duke or classical music at St George's. Bristol does not yet have an arena to host the biggest touring acts, but in 2020 plans were well underway to transform three huge former aircraft hangars in Filton into the YTL Arena.

Completely on the other side of the music venue spectrum from an arena is the Exchange, with not only two event spaces hosting everything from thrash metal gigs to talks and conferences, but also a coffee shop and kitchen, record shop, recording studio, and office space for local promoters and record labels. The Exchange became Bristol's first community-owned venue in January 2019 after it hit its fundraising target of £250,000 with just days to spare. Music fans across Bristol and further afield are now co-owners of the venue, which puts on live music as often as seven nights a week, with bands like Bristol's own Idles and former Bristol student George Ezra earning their stripes here before going on to play festival main stages across the world.

The depth of love for the Exchange was exemplified on a chilly Friday night in 2018 when DJ Michael Savage played 'Africa' by Toto on a loop for 12 hours, from 11pm to 11am the next day. Music lovers were sponsored to see how long they could bear listening to the echoing of the drums, with their feat of endurance raising funds for Temwa, a Bristol-based charity working to develop self-sufficient communities in remote rural areas of northern Malawi.

Address 72-73 Old Market Street, Old Market, BS2 0EJ, info@exchangebristol.com, www.exchangebristol.com | **Getting there** 2-minute walk from Castle Park; opposite Old Market Street bus stops | **Hours** Coffee shop open Mon–Fri 7.30am–6pm, Sat & Sun 10am–6pm. Check listings for venue opening times | **Tip** Opposite the Exchange is No. 25A, a cafe that might just take the crown for the best cheese toasties in Bristol, as well as serving great coffee and selling a number of locally brewed beers (www.instagram.com/25a_oldmarket).

48_Felix Road Playground

Get the kids outdoors!

Imagine a world of infinite possibility. Well, a world of infinite possibility if you are a child under a certain height. Felix Road Adventure Playground is hidden among the residential streets of the Easton neighbourhood in east Bristol, and now counts among its regular visitors mums and dads who played here when they were young and now bring their own children. Turn your back and you may see your seven-year-old climbing up a ladder to the top of a shipping container and jumping off onto a crash mat below, put there by a helpful adult. In an age when children too often remain indoors on their iPads, this is a place of mostly outdoor fun, where taking risks is positively encouraged, and youngsters return home with their clothes smelling of bonfires and their heads full of plans for their next adventure.

Felix Road was established as a play provision by a group of keen volunteers in 1972. After a period managed in partnership with Bristol City Council, it is now run by the community for the community, priding itself on being dedicated to children's play, family time and community togetherness.

Children have a wide range of play possibilities – supervised at all times by qualified playworkers – including large wooden structures, tree houses, rope and tyre swings, a zip line, climbing beams, and nets. The main wooden structure has grown in size over the years and looks a bit like Bristol Wood Recycling Project's yard (see ch. 24) would if paths had been created through its ever-changing stock for little people to career through at will with no regard for draconian health and safety regulations. There is also a stage, a football pitch and a pizza oven. It's not just outdoor activities either, with a sensory room and a music room. Arrive on the right day and you'll find some of the best-value curries in Bristol being served from the kitchen.

Address Felix Road, Easton, BS5 0JW, +44 (0)117 902 2222, info.felixroad@gmail.com, www.felixroad.uk | Getting there 2-minute walk from the bus stop on corner of Stapleton Road and Villiers Road, 10-minute walk from Stapleton Road railway station | Hours Mon–Thu 3.30–5.30pm (term time), noon–5.30pm (school holidays), Sun & bank holidays Mon 1–5pm | Tip If you are in charge of children who need to let off more steam, one of Bristol's biggest and best playgrounds is at Blaise Castle Estate. When you've had enough of the playground, explore the 650-acre grounds and don't miss nearby Blaise Hamlet (www.nationaltrust.org.uk/blaise-hamlet).

49 Folk House

From working folk to folk music

If you have always wanted to learn how to practise the ancient Chinese exercise of qi gong, make your own teapot on a potter's wheel or get help writing your first novel, then Bristol Folk House is the place for you. Dozens of creative courses in a huge variety of subjects, from photography to drama, languages to interior design, are held here throughout the week, with one-day workshops as well as part-time day and evening classes for over-18s. It also hosts folk (of course), roots and acoustic music at weekends, dance events, and is a regular venue for music festivals. This place is clearly much more than just an adult education centre.

What is now the Folk House can trace its history back to a men's club founded on Deanery Road in 1887 on the site of the current Central Library (see ch. 21). The club provided local working men with an option that wasn't the pub; a place where they could spend their leisure time learning to read and write rather than drinking another pint of mild: 'good husbands and fathers... sober, honest, industrious men who use their brains and are good citizens' were the target, according to an early mission statement. In 1920, the Folk House was established on the same site with a programme of activities and classes for men and women. The present building hidden just off Park Street was opened in 1964 and it has been run as a cooperative since 1996.

Today, there is as much chance of wandering in on a discussion of classical literature, members of a guitar class just finishing a jam or people crouched over their black-and-white photos being developed in a dark room, as there would have been when the organisation was founded. But there is also the likes of burlesque classes and digital photography, life drawing and mindful yoga. And it's no longer frowned upon to drink beer, with cans from Bristol breweries available from the fridge in the on-site cafe.

Address 40a Park Street, BS1 5JG, +44 (0)117 926 2987, admin@bristolfolkhouse.co.uk, www.bristolfolkhouse.co.uk | Getting there Take a narrow alleyway towards the middle of Park Street, on your right if going up the hill; 3-minute walk from College Green | Hours Mon–Thu 9am–9pm, Fri & Sat 9am–5pm | Tip The other side of Park Street from the Folk House is Brandon Hill, a wonderful green space topped by Cabot Tower, which you can climb for panoramic views.

50 Friendly Records

A vinyl revival

When Bristol band-of-the-moment Idles performed an incendiary set at Glastonbury Festival in 2019, drummer Jon Beavis played in a Friendly Records vest. It was a subtle nod of appreciation to the small independent record shop in Bedminster that sells new and used vinyl but, in the words of co-owner Tom Friend (yes, that's his real name), they 'are deliberately not defined by any particular genre. We just try and stock good music, mostly what we like, in the hope that other people will like it too!' Friendly Records grew out of Tom's expanding music collection and the shop has since branched out into the bar he owns next door, which sells the reduced-price records that cannot fit into the main shop and where DJs play vinyl-only sets.

If you want to replicate Idles' look at Glastonbury, there are vests for sale as well as t-shirts, hoodies, bags and caps. A pair of original posters on one wall are for a groundbreaking graffiti exhibition that took place in the Arnolfini art gallery in 1985, featuring a young 3D, who later co-founded Massive Attack. Records here cost from around £10 and are divided by genre (New Zealand indie, anyone?) with a particular emphasis on soundtracks, including many from Bristol's own Invada Records. A recent rummage unearthed the likes of *Bait*, produced by Bristol-based Early Day Films, and Netflix's *Stranger Things*.

More rummaging reveals a glimpse of Bristol music history, with The Bristol Recorder compilation recorded live at the former Carwardine's on Corn Street in September 1980 having small adverts on its front sleeve for a much-missed record shop, Revolver on the Clifton Triangle, and former punk record label Fried Egg Records. Tom wants his shop not just to stock records but also to be about community and meeting people, where you can bump into a friend that you haven't seen for a while. You can't do that while shopping online.

Address 59 North Street, Bedminster, BS3 1ES, +44 (0)117 239 7169, www.friendlyrecords.co.uk | **Getting there** 10-minute walk from Wapping Wharf; bus 24 to North Street | **Hours** Tue–Sat noon–6pm, Sun noon–4pm | **Tip** Almost next door is the superb Storysmith bookshop, which as well as its packed shelves of books also serves good coffee and hosts regular literary events (www.storysmithbooks.com).

51 — Glitch

A passion for innovation

Why just cut people's hair when you can also sell house plants? And why just cut people's hair and sell house plants when you can also serve coffee, host live music and sell records? Glitch is one of those undefinable businesses in Bristol doing a variety of different but complementary things under the same roof, and it is always evolving. There was previously a nail bar here, Gossip, which has now moved a few hundred yards up the road; former kitchen residents Grano are now based in To the Moon, again nearby, where they serve delicious traditional Italian food. The Old Market community continues to grow and develop, and former tenants here often don't want to move too far from their loyal customers.

This corner building is a former shop and stockroom knocked together, with bare concrete floors and breezeblocks still visible on one section of wall now acting as a backdrop for cacti, succulents and strings of hearts. Underneath a neon sign spelling out 'I'm a Glitch bitch' is the basket of resident dog Alfie, content to watch the world go by around him.

Current kitchen residents Coffee & Vinyl moved into their half of the building at the beginning of 2020 after opening their first cafe in Torquay on the Devon coast. Coffee is for sale here at their Bristol outpost alongside some mighty fine cakes, with vinyl records on shelves in one corner of the salon. It is yet more strings to the bow of Glitch, which was the dream of owner Stephan Vi, who based the concept on a creative hub that he had set up in his native Florence in Italy.

A well-known Bristol poet arrived in Glitch to have his hair cut on a chilly Friday morning, steering his wheelchair down the slope between the cafe-cum-waiting area and the salon, through the mini jungle of plants. 'I don't really know what this is,' he said, taking in his surroundings. 'But we're so lucky to have it in Bristol.'

Address 48-49 Old Market Street, Old Market, BS2 0EX, +44 (0)7340 235 380,
www.weareglitch.com | Getting there 2-minute walk from Old Market Street bus
stops, 7-minute walk from Cabot Circus | Hours Tue, Wed & Fri 10am–7pm,
Thu & Sat 10am–6pm | Tip Life of Si at 80 West Street is another special part of
Old Market. The shop sells books, advertising art, maps, prints, ephemera and more,
collected over a lifetime by owner Simon Ellis, who is also a regular at Bristol markets
(www.facebook.com/LifeofSimonEllis).

52 Goat Gully
Hairy conservationists

There are some surprising members of the local community to thank for their hard work making room for rare wildflowers on this steep slope from the Downs to the Avon Gorge. These hairy conservationists do not receive any monetary payment, and are simply content to eat invasive plants like scrub and bramble. In a botanically rich part of the Gorge known as the Gully, trees and scrub had been removed by conservation workers and some of the grasslands had started to recover. But this work could only be carried out in the winter, and controlling the scrubby re-growth was a constant, labour-intensive battle. So the project began to look for a more sustainable solution. Enter the goats.

Feral billy goats were chosen as they naturally prefer to eat scrubby, woody vegetation rather than grasses and wildflowers, and they also suit the steep and difficult terrain. Six Kashmir goats arrived from north Wales in 2011 and were introduced into a fenced enclosure. Since then, their grazing has opened the area up, giving the rare plants and insects a chance to thrive. The animals are checked every day, with regular 'meet the goat keeper' walks organised as well as education sessions explaining the goats' role in helping to conserve the rare plants of the Gorge.

In 2015, a set of Victorian steps was restored from the top of the gully down to the bottom. It takes you down next to a monument commemorating a storm drain on one side of the Portway, which in Victorian times was a much more pleasant place to promenade than today. Walk down the steps and you will pass a ventilation shaft for the Severn Beach railway line (see ch. 94), which runs between Clifton Down and Sea Mills stations in a tunnel deep below where you are walking. The journey down the steps and scree is steep, and sturdy footwear is advised if you want to be as sure-footed as the resident goats.

Address Clifton Downs, BS9 1FG, www.avongorge.org.uk | **Getting there** 15-minute walk from Clifton Suspension Bridge, accessed via a path off Circular Road | **Hours** Unrestricted | **Tip** If you want a guarantee of seeing animals, visit Bristol Zoo. Home to lions, gorillas and a variety of smaller creatures, it also supports conservation and research projects across the world (www.bristolzoo.org.uk).

53 Goldney Hall Grotto

A subterranean treasure

Anybody who has watched *Sherlock* will recognise the orangery at Goldney Hall as the venue for John Watson and Mary Morstan's wedding in the third season of the BBC show. Goldney Hall's orangery – which is used for real as well as fictional weddings – dates back to 1714 when it was first built as a greenhouse for Thomas Goldney II (1664–1731), a Quaker merchant who made his fortune through investing in privateering voyages. As Goldney's garden grew, he began the construction of the subterranean grotto, its most intricate and intriguing feature. Measuring some 36 feet long by 12 feet wide, the grotto's chamber is made up of three halls divided by columns decorated with 'Bristol diamonds', the colloquial name for the iron-rich quartz found around the city. Much of the grotto was formed from Brandon Hill grit, a deep-red sandstone quarried only a few hundred yards away. Goldney's initials are written in shells by the skylight closest to the entrance.

A pair of lions carved from Bath stone guard the entrance to the grotto. To the left, the east chamber contains a pool filled by a cascade overlooked by a river god holding a gushing urn who is also made from Bath stone. On the right, the west chamber contains niches around the walls on which to sit. Lit by skylights, the whole cavern is decorated with a combination of carved Bath stone, minerals, ammonites, and more than 200 species of shells and coral. After a visit in 1756, grotto expert Mary Delany declared, 'The walls on each hand are richly, irregularly and very boldly adorned with everything the earth and sea can produce proper for the purpose, all in their highest perfection… it is by much the finest thing of the kind I ever saw.'

The University of Bristol took ownership of the house and gardens in 1956, with Goldney Hall now much sought-after as undergraduate accommodation.

Address Lower Clifton Hill, Clifton, BS8 1BX | **Getting there** A few minutes' walk from the bus 8 stop at Victoria Square, or the U2 stop on Jacob's Wells Road | **Hours** Usually closed to the public; look out for tours organised by the University, special events like the annual Amnesty International garden party and outdoor cinema screenings – or get invited to a wedding | **Tip** Birdcage Walk is a beautiful arched walkway that stretches from Clifton Hill opposite Goldney Hall to Victoria Square. It is all that remains of the 12th-century St Andrew's Church, built in the 12th century and destroyed in the Bristol Blitz.

54_ Guilbert's

Home to Bristol's own Oompa Loompas

Push open the door of Guilbert's and a bell sounds to bring somebody from the hidden chocolate-making area to serve you in the shop. A member of staff will usually arrive at the counter still with a hairnet on, interrupted from following cherished recipes that have been handed down through the generations.

Guilbert's was first opened on Park Street in 1910 by Swiss immigrant Piers Guilbert, who soon opened a second shop on Milsom Street in Bath. During World War II the Park Street shop was bombed and the business moved to Leonard Lane, and from there to Small Street opposite Bristol Crown Court. Today, its proud heritage continues in the heart of the Old City in what is believed to be the oldest building in Bristol still in commercial use. What is now Guilbert's was once the house of John Foster, a former mayor of Bristol and founder in 1483 of Foster's Almshouse on Colston Street close to the top of Christmas Steps, now converted to private homes.

Still family-owned, Guilbert's pride themselves on their traditional methods. There are no mechanised production lines here, with all of the chocolates hand-dipped by their own team of Oompa Loompas. Behind the scenes are shelves of metal moulds that have been for decades used in the creation of seasonal items such as Easter eggs. Front of house, choose from a delicious selection always on display, 'using fresh, quality, preservative-free ingredients which are still entirely handmade with expertise, excellence and above all, passion'. Your choices might include the likes of orange creams, Turkish delight and colourful crystallised fondants. Or will you brave the blackberry absinthe truffle? Find chocolate candy buttons in a variety of flavours, metal commemorative tins, selection boxes and solid bars of some of the best chocolate in Bristol, and certainly with the proudest history.

Address 16-17 Small Street, BS1 1DE, +44 (0)117 926 8102, info@guilbertschocolates.co.uk, www.guilbertschocolates.co.uk | Getting there 2-minute walk from St Nick's Market | Hours Mon–Fri 7.30am–4.30pm, Sat 10am–3pm (Nov & Dec only) | Tip Just a few doors down is Small Street Espresso, Bristol's original speciality coffee shop (www.smallstreetespresso.co.uk). On nearby Broad Street is Full Court Press, where good coffee is taken even more seriously (fcp.coffee).

55 Hart's Bakery

From bondage to bread

Laura Hart began selling baked goods from the back of her bicycle. After being the in-house baker at a number of Bristol restaurants, she established her first bakery up a rickety staircase off Whiteladies Road. Following a search of more than a year, she opened her first permanent premises in an arch underneath Temple Meads rumoured to have once been a bondage parlour. From the ovens within the archway now come an ever-changing selection of breads, pastries, biscuits and cakes under the guidance of Laura and her husband Pete, formerly an engineer at Dyson. Hart's is certainly not the only Bristol business based in railway archways. Around Temple Meads, find a bike shop, a gym and even a cider-maker going about their day as trains pass overhead.

Laura has always wanted her business to be a bakery first and a cafe second, with customers either eating in or grabbing and going, able to watch the bakers at work in the open kitchen. In the morning, pastries are ready before the first customers arrive, with lunch specials – that might include Cornish pasties, savoury tarts and pies – placed straight onto the counter once out of the oven. You will quickly find your own favourites, but be sure to try the custard tarts and cinnamon buns.

For many, this bakery is the beating heart of Bristol's food scene. Laura has not forgotten the beginnings of her business, with regular 'Starts at Hart's' events seeing the forecourt given over to new businesses selling everything from pot plants to panniers. The bakery also plays host to regular supper clubs as well as giving artists the opportunity to exhibit on its walls. Each December heralds the arrival of their marvellous mince pies with a crumble topping. And if you have a train to catch from Temple Meads at any time of the year, it's always worth arriving at the station early to stock up for the best train picnic ever.

Address 35 Lower Approach Road, BS1 6QS, +44 (0)117 992 4488, laura@hartsbakery.co.uk, www.hartsbakery.co.uk | Getting there Directly under the Temple Meads forecourt, down the staircase near the British Transport Police office, or along Lower Approach Road from Temple Gate | Hours Tue–Sat 7am–3pm | Tip On the other side of Temple Meads is Yurt Lush, a cafe and bar in adjoining Mongolian yurts (www.yurtlush.co.uk). Another archway hosts the Loco Klub, which features some of Bristol's most eclectic events (www.locobristol.com).

56   Henleaze Lake

Swim in a former quarry

One of Bristol's most exclusive enclaves is a club and also a charity that is enjoyed by swimmers and anglers as much as its resident wildlife. Open-water swimming is the primary use of Henleaze Lake but fishing also takes place here throughout the year. It's a long way away from the 19th century when this site was one of a number of limestone quarries in the Southmead area. Sometime after 1903, this particular quarry ceased production, was allowed to flood, and soon afterwards started to be used for swimming in the warmer months and ice-skating when the water froze over. The surroundings may still have been bucolic in the lake's early days, but it was also a dangerous place. In 1908, a Royal Humane Society gold medal was awarded to a Mr Turner who after his morning dip rescued a struggling fellow swimmer.

There was a drowning here when it was still known as Shellard's Quarry, and drownings in both 1916 and 1917 put a stop to swimming and a club established under strict rules so that swimming could be safely resumed.

Henleaze Swimming Club took over the management of the lake, with not just swimming but also water polo, lifesaving and diving competitions. The club continues to thrive today with a long waiting list. Surrounded by lawns and trees, the lake is fed by spring water and is about 400 metres long and between 30 and 60 metres wide, with a steep rock face on one side and a wooded bank on the other. There are two springboards, two fixed diving boards and the opportunity to spot moorhens, mallards, herons and kingfishers. Swimming takes place all year round even in the coldest water temperatures, with a sauna particularly popular as the thermometer approaches zero. If you can't make friends with a member and be taken here as their guest, the lake is also used for training for triathlons, open-water events and Channel swimming.

Address Lake Road, Henleaze, BS10 5HG, +44 (0)117 962 0696, administration@henleazeswimmingclub.org, www.henleazeswimmingclub.org | Getting there Buses 20, 21, 54, 54B all stop nearby | Hours The lake is open to members and their guests only. Regular public tours were due to start in 2020. | Tip Badock's Wood between Henleaze and Southmead is a small nature reserve providing an urban haven for wildlife. The site was given to the city in 1937 by local industrialist Sir Stanley Badock (www.fobw.org.uk).

57 The High Cross
Can we have it back please?

At the junction of High Street, Corn Street, Broad Street and Wine Street once stood the 14th-century High Cross. It marked the centre of medieval Bristol, with these roads radiating out to the main gates within the city wall. The High Cross was just one of many crosses in Bristol associated with ancient churches, but none of them remain. The upper parts of a near-replica High Cross, sculpted in 1851, have been here on Berkeley Square since 1956, but more squirrels than people pass it every day. You can find it weather-beaten and chipped in an often-muddy corner of the square, which is a popular lunch spot for office workers and students in the summer.

The original limestone High Cross was gilded and coloured, presumably once making for a splendid sight. Within niches were statues of Kings John, Henry III, Edward III and Edward IV – all of whom had contributed to Bristol's expansion and trade by conferring important charters. More monarchs were added when the cross was repaired and enlarged in the 17th century, and painted blue and gold.

The High Cross was removed from its original location in 1733 due to the concerns of an evidently influential resident on the corner of Wine Street and High Street, who claimed that his house and life were in danger every time the wind blew. The cross was re-erected on College Green, where it was soon declared a 'nuisance' by locals who were early practitioners of one of Bristol's favourite pastimes of nimbyism (Not In My Back Yard). After being dismantled and stored in the cathedral, in 1764 it was transported on six wagons to Stourhead in Wiltshire, where it still remains as a picturesque attraction in the garden of the country estate. Picturesque it may be, but every so often there is talk of ensuring its long hoped-for return to Bristol, where the stumped replica is no substitute for the real thing.

Address Berkeley Square, Clifton, BS8 1HB | **Getting there** 2-minute walk from Clifton Triangle | **Hours** Unrestricted | **Tip** Bristol Museum & Art Gallery has one gallery dedicated to maps of the city, with the High Cross seen on the earliest surviving map of an English town. Elusive Bristol street artist Banksy had an exhibition here in 2009 which remained secret to even the staff until the day of its opening (www.bristolmuseums.org.uk/bristol-museum-and-art-gallery).

58 High Kingsdown
A low-rise architectural marvel

When recommending that High Kingsdown be granted the status of a Conservation Area in 1994, just two decades after it was built, a senior architectural investigator for English Heritage noted that the area 'was an entirely pedestrianised piece of total townscape that is exceptional on such a scale'.

High Kingsdown is situated in an area that developed during the 18th and early 19th centuries, but was badly damaged by bombing during World War II and left dilapidated. The area was first proposed for demolition in 1957 but initial proposals for three large tower blocks met with vehement local and national protests. Alternative plans put forward by architects Whicheloe Macfarlane were a smaller version of an initially much larger scheme, with 400 dwellings scaled down to what is today just over 100 houses. The homes, grouped mostly in zigzags of three and four, are indebted to traditional Danish housing but also to traditional Chinese and Islamic models.

Even the particular colour of green that the garage doors must be painted are specified in the deeds, with an active residents association tending communal flowerbeds, picking litter and in 2018 leading the refurbishment of the central playground known to many children as the 'soldier playground' because of the small red-uniformed metal soldiers around its perimeter. Being so close to the University of Bristol campus, many of the houses here are unsurprisingly occupied by students. A block of flats five storeys high, originally built for the elderly, is now student accommodation, as is the former Victorian-era King's Arms pub that was at the heart of the plans for the original 1970s' estate. A growing number of permanent residents now fear that despite the various benefits that the university brings, this special area will lose its soul if it becomes even more dominated by such a transient population.

Address High Kingsdown, Kingsdown, BS2 8EN, www.highkingsdown.co.uk | Getting there 15-minute walk from Stokes Croft; bus 9 or 72 to St Michael's Hill, or bus 77 to Montague Place | Hours Unrestricted | Tip None of the coffee beans for sale in TwoDay Coffee Roasters on St Michael's Hill opposite High Kingsdown are older than two days after roasting. When you buy them here you can also grab a coffee to go or restock on Aeropress filters (www.twodaycoffee.co.uk).

59 Horfield Common Urinal

A Moorish-style men's room

Bristol has a habit of giving former toilets a new lease of life, most often with cafes setting up in their place, for example Cafe on the Square in Sea Mills, Cafe Retreat next to the water tower on the Downs and Cloakroom Cafe on Park Row. A particularly memorable time in former public conveniences was had underneath Prince Street during the Bristol Harbour Festival in 2015 when it was turned into a giant ball pit soundtracked by live DJs. Afterwards, it was sadly concreted up and the iron railings at its two entrances removed to make way for a new bus stop and segregated cycle lane on the road above.

Unfortunately, Bristol now has more former toilets than toilets still in use following the council's decision in 2017 to close more than a dozen across the city in order to cut costs. A community toilet scheme now sees businesses open their own facilities to the public – with City Hall, the M Shed, Colston Hall and the Create Centre among those whose toilets are available.

There certainly aren't many toilets across the UK that are also Grade II-listed buildings, but another former toilet on the corner of Horfield Common has this distinction, as well as having an identical twin in Mina Road Park in St Werburgh's, and a close relative on display next to the SS *Great Britain*. Built in the late 19th century in Glasgow from cast iron, the round, racing-green urinal has a curved entrance screen, decorative pierced panels and a Moorish-style dome on top.

It has been listed since 1977 and is a rare surviving example of a once common type of building among Bristol's streetscape. An English Heritage spokesperson described a similar toilet at the top of Blackboy Hill in Clifton, which gained listed status in 2014, as representative of the 'civic aspirations of the authorities in the Bristol suburbs in the late Victorian period'.

Address Gloucester Road, Horfield, BS7 8UR | Getting there Bus 75 or 76 to Horfield Common | Hours Unrestricted | Tip The Bath Ales-owned Wellington pub by the Horfield Common toilet is a popular stop for Bristol Rovers fans before a game at the nearby Memorial Stadium. Have a pint downstairs and stay in one of the ten hotel-style bedrooms upstairs (www.thewellingtonbristol.co.uk).

60__Incredible Edible
Growing food on street corners

On any given day in Bristol, you might walk by a small group of people gardening within a sunken roundabout (see ch. 10), on a station platform or the corner of a public square. Where before was just concrete or dirt, more than 50 edible gardens have now been planted across the city by Incredible Edible volunteers and partners. The food is free for anyone to take as well as providing meals for pollinators, birds and other creatures who are part of Bristol's ecosystem. A typical work party session might include pruning a passion fruit tree or training Japanese quinces. Chalk noticeboards then let passers-by know when the items can be eaten.

Since 2014 – the year before Bristol became European Green Capital – Incredible Edible have been on a mission to inspire people to take food production back into their own hands. It is now possible to walk by a series of more than a dozen gardens that lead from Temple Meads to Millennium Square. The first bed created as part of this Food Growing Trail was planted on platform three of Temple Meads, but growing conditions were difficult so it was moved outside near the entrance to The Passenger Shed (see ch. 76), with a rhubarb plant and a blackcurrant bush its first occupants. On Station Approach, almost above the arch containing Hart's Bakery (see ch. 55) is another bed with strawberries and a dwarf nectarine tree that has so far fruited every year. A fruit garden with the likes of quince, gooseberries and redcurrants can be found in front of St Mary Redcliffe church; while there is a herb garden on Anchor Square with lavender, rosemary, thyme and more.

Organisations who work with Incredible Edible include Good Gym (www.goodgym.org), whose Tuesday group runs see members stretch their legs to head out to help community projects, before running back to the start at Workout Bristol gym on Welsh Back, all within 90 minutes.

On the placard:

Bug-Ingham Palace

Address Various locations, info@ediblebristol.org.uk, www.ediblebristol.org.uk | Hours Unrestricted | Tip Close to Incredible Edible's flowerbeds on Millennium Square is a silver ball housing the only 3D planetarium in the UK. It's part of We The Curious, the perfect place to spend a day at the intersection between science, art, people and ideas (www.wethecurious.org).

61 Ken Stradling Collection

One man's passion for beautiful objects

The Ken Stradling Collection is a treasure trove of items amassed from a lifetime of collecting that tells the story not just of one man's passion for beautiful and unusual objects, but also the story of objects from this century and the last.

It was back in 1948 that Ken joined the Bristol Guild of Applied Arts. During his career at the shop and art gallery that remains a popular destination on Park Street, he was a buyer, manager and director, finding and selling new and innovative furnishings and objects for homes across Bristol. At the same time, he also began his own collection of 20th- and 21st-century objects. This very personal hoard now forms the basis of the Ken Stradling Collection, open to the public and hosting regularly changing exhibitions exploring the collection itself and related subjects. Recent exhibitions have included celebrating the centenary of the influential Bauhaus school of architecture and design, ceramics from Cardiff School of Art & Design, and British studio pottery from the 1950s and 1960s. The wider collection is housed across three floors with visits able to be arranged by appointment.

48 Park Row is also home to the Design Study Centre, a resource of objects and documentary material for anyone with an interest in design, with developing links to universities and art schools across the UK.

The collection contains more than 500 pieces of studio ceramics, 200 pieces of Scandinavian and British studio glass, as well as many items of furniture, industrial design, decorative objects, paintings and prints. It demonstrates a decades-long fascination with the making of domestic objects, an aim to present and promote good design, and a love of sharing it with others. Ken's lifetime commitment to his craft was honoured when he was awarded an MBE for services to the arts in Bristol in the 2020 New Year Honours list.

Address 48 Park Row, BS1 5LH, +44 (0)117 3290 566, info@stradlingcollection.org, www.stradlingcollection.org | Getting there 2-minute walk from Park Street | Hours Wed 11am–4pm, Sat (during exhibitions) 11am–4pm | Tip Next door is Hobbs Hairdressing, run by the inimitable Doug Hobbs, who also organises the annual Hobbs Show featuring fashion, dancing, music and more, raising money for charity. In the summer you can sit in the secret garden tended by Doug and his team (www.hobbs-style.co.uk).

62 Kiln Restaurant

Once the hottest place in town

Looking at illustrated panoramas of bygone Bristol, it's hard to find familiar silhouettes of buildings other than churches. The view is more pastoral, with fields where there are now houses; the tall masts of ships stand like a forest of trees right along the docks into the heart of the city. One other astonishing difference from then to the present day is the number of structures that look like upside-down ice cream cones. When the poet Alexander Pope visited Bristol in 1739, he counted 20 such cones, 'smoking over the town'. These were kilns that used to belch thick smoke, and were used in the manufacture of both glass and pottery. Bristol was once the UK's largest glass-making centre outside of London, with the industry centred around Redcliffe where fine sand needed in its production was mined.

Reminders of this era have all but gone, and the only surviving structure from Bristol's glass industry can be found on Prewett Street. Built between 1773 and 1812, it replaced an earlier cone from the 17th century and was originally 46 metres (150 feet) high. The site was later incorporated into a chemical works and used as a chemical store until shortly before World War II, when the cone was reduced in height due to the deterioration of its brickwork. The top was removed and a roof of corrugated sheeting put over it before the truncated cone became a restaurant in the 1970s as part of the new Dragonara Hotel – owners Ladbrokes making the unusual decision for the time of converting rather than demolishing.

In its early days, the restaurant won culinary acclaim and was a place to be seen, with bands such as Thin Lizzy and visiting football and cricket teams also passing through the hotel. Today, the Kiln serves unadventurous culinary fare such as beef burgers, herb crusted racks of English lamb and cheesecake within its unique historic surroundings.

Address Doubletree by Hilton, Redcliffe Way, Redcliffe, BS1 6NJ, +44 (0)117 926 0041, www.doubletree3.hilton.com | Getting there 3-minute walk from Temple Meads | Hours Breakfast Mon–Fri 6.30–9.30am, Sat & Sun 7–10.30am; dinner Mon–Sat 6–10pm | Tip Another restaurant in Redcliffe, Casamia, is regularly named among the best in the UK. Holder of a Michelin star since 2009, its tasting menus change seasonally (www.casamiarestaurant.co.uk).

63 Kings Weston Roman Villa

Marooned Roman remains

Now located in the middle of a post-war housing estate, Kings Weston Roman villa was once the home of a wealthy Roman family. The villa – which features the only Roman bath suite in Bristol and original mosaic floors – was discovered during the construction of the Lawrence Weston estate in 1947 and can now be accessed by borrowing a key from nearby Blaise Castle Museum.

Unlike in neighbouring Bath, there was no major Roman settlement in Bristol. The site of a small farm was discovered on Upper Maudlin Street in the city centre, with another agricultural site excavated in Bedminster, and other villas in Brislington and Keynsham. In the Roman period, the major Roman settlement in Bristol was Abona on a bend of the River Avon, where Sea Mills is located today. It was likely to have been originally of military origin, with a civilian town established around it by the early second century. Abona was linked to Bath by a Roman road whose remains can still be seen on the Downs between Stoke Bishop and Clifton.

The villa at Kings Weston was a mile away from Abona and has been dated to the end of the third century, thanks to coins found there. The modern Long Cross road partially destroyed it, with two buildings discovered but only the eastern one excavated and conserved. The almost symmetrical building had a number of structural features including decorated wall plaster and mosaic floors. David Higgins, former head of the department of Italian studies at the University of Bristol, writes that compared to others, this villa is 'not at all impressive as to size or architectural elaboration', but it is likely that it was once at the centre of a villa estate, with the family living in it controlling satellite rural settlements. Its demise came around 367 AD with the west wing burnt down, possibly at the hands of Irish raiders.

Address Long Cross, Lawrence Weston, BS11 0LP | **Getting there** Bus 4 to Long Cross | **Hours** For unescorted visits, pick up a key from Blaise Museum or Bristol Museum & Art Gallery for a £10 refundable deposit | **Tip** Nearby Kings Weston House is a Grade I-listed building designed by Sir John Vanbrugh, who also designed Blenheim Palace (www.kingswestonhouse.co.uk).

64 Knowle West Media Centre

Made of straw, but solid as a rock

Released in 2008, *Knowle West Boy* is the seventh studio album from regular Massive Attack collaborator Tricky, named after the area of Bristol in which he grew up. 'You're into chaos. Like I,' he told one pupil at his old school in a visit captured by a documentary film crew. Chaos of a very different type is part of the story of Ellis Genge, an England rugby player who also grew up in Knowle West and during the truncated 2020 Six Nations tournament fought a one-man war on rugby snobbery.

Knowle West can best be described as a deprived but tightly knit suburb, with the Knowle West Media Centre (KWMC) an arts centre and charity that has been based at the heart of this south Bristol estate since 1996. Its origins can be traced back to a photography project run by Carolyn Hassan, now the KWMC director, who with her team went on to run other projects in the area out of a former health centre. KWMC is now based in a purpose-built building partly constructed from straw bales. But even more interesting than the environmental sustainability of the building is what happens inside it.

'At Knowle West Media Centre we support people to make positive changes in their lives and communities, using technology and the arts to come up with creative solutions to problems and explore new ways of doing things,' says the KWMC website. That is what they do in a nutshell, with recent projects based around music, film and photography, and local issues. And then there is The Factory in nearby Filwood Green Business Park, a space for making, digital fabrication and product design that also offers training and enterprise support. One successful project here involves taking old office furniture and using local labour to revive it for modern workspaces. It may all sound like chaos, but it is making Knowle West an area to be proud of.

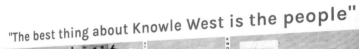

"The best thing about Knowle West is the people"

Address Leinster Avenue, Knowle West, BS4 1NL, +44 (0)117 903 0444,
enquiries@kwmc.org.uk, www.kwmc.org.uk | Getting there Bus 91 to Broadbury Road
just across the road from KWMC, or bus 90 to Donegal Road, a 5-minute walk away |
Hours Reception open Mon–Fri 9am–5pm | Tip Also on Filwood Green Business Park
is Temple Cycles, the creators of Bristol's most beautiful bikes (www.templecycles.co.uk).

65 Letterpress Collective
An ancient trade revived

Walk down Leonard Lane, past the street art of varying ability on either side of this narrow thoroughfare that still follows its medieval route, and you will come across a small blue bridge above your head. The corrugated-iron bridge used to connect the *Bristol Times and Mirror* newspaper offices on St Stephen's Street (now a backpackers hostel) to the printing presses in what is now Centrespace Gallery. Inside, the ancient art of printing continues at the Letterpress Collective. Some of the machines still in everyday use here are old enough to be in museums, with founder Nick Hand (one of only two full-time members of staff) gathering together wood and lead type dating back several centuries. There's also a collection of printing presses including the Heildelberg Platen Press machine – known for its windmill-like automatic paper-feed mechanism – made in Germany in 1960 and winched out of the M Shed museum's store by a dockside crane.

Nick sees the business as a chance to learn from the last of the printers and compositors in the city so that a new generation can understand and learn the thrill of working a small press and seeing your creation in ink on paper. Nick himself has travelled from Land's End to John O'Groats, around Ireland and the USA, on a bicycle with a printing press on the back, printing thousands of postcards along the way from the factories and workshops of fellow makers and craftspeople.

Patience is needed for the limited-edition print jobs here, with Nick and his colleague Ellen Bills running one-day workshops and evening classes so other people can get a glimpse into their trade. Look out for special events such as a 'wayzgoose', a name since medieval times for a gathering of letterpress printers, where they sell beautiful printed objects and Wilding cider from Somerset – with the labels handmade here of course.

Address 6 Leonard Lane, BS1 1EA, hello@theletterpresscollective.org, theletterpresscollective.org | Getting there 2-minute walk from St Nick's Market | Hours Mon 9am–5pm, Tue–Fri 8am–6pm | Tip Centrespace Gallery was founded in 2000 and is an independent exhibition space hosting a variety of events throughout the year as well as offering studios to artists, craftspeople and creatives (www.centrespacegallery.com).

66 Lollypop-Be-Bop

A little bit of magic

The story behind the appearance of a secret plaque is as magical and mysterious as the events that it describes. The plaque, which was stuck to a low wall outside Bristol Children's Hospital in 2014 by Cormac Seachoy, reads: 'Dedicated to the children of Bristol, the 1998 Quidditch World Cup Posts, enchanted by Adou Sosseh. Have a magical day!' Anybody who has read the Harry Potter books or seen the films will know that quidditch is a game wizards play on broomsticks, and the sculpture in front of the hospital looks remarkably similar to quidditch goalposts. But it would take a serious Potter fan to know that Sosseh was captain of the Senegal team which lost the 1998 Quidditch World Cup to Malawi – a 'fact' J. K. Rowling only revealed on the Pottermore website.

Looking for contributions to his crowdfunding campaign, Cormac wrote: 'I thought it would be an awesome idea to somehow convey to Bristol that the sculpture is actually the quidditch posts from the 1998 World Cup and that they have been enchanted into place as a gift from wizards to the Bristol Children's Hospital. So I bought a really classy and permanent cast bronze plaque, got it engraved with a dedication message, and it's going to be stuck to the wall beneath the sculpture at the start of December as a Christmas gift to the hospital.'

Sadly, less than a year after he installed the plaque, Cormac was diagnosed with terminal cancer and died aged just 27.

These quidditch posts are in fact an 18-metre-high interactive sculpture called *Lollypop-Be-Bop* by artist Andrew Smith. It was commissioned to accompany the 2001 opening of a new building. As well as providing a welcoming and fun face to nervous children arriving at the hospital, a steel console inside the building has buttons corresponding to each of the coloured rings of the sculpture. Press any button to hear music and sounds created by children.

DEDICATED
TO THE
CHILDREN OF BRISTOL
THE
1998 QUIDDITCH WORLD CUP
POSTS
ENCHANTED BY ADOU SOSSEH

HAVE A MAGICAL DAY!

Address Bristol Royal Hospital for Children, Upper Maudlin Street, BS2 8BJ, www.uhbw.nhs.uk | **Getting there** 2-minute walk from top of Christmas Steps | **Hours** Unrestricted | **Tip** Southmead Hospital has a number of lifesize bronze sculptures of injured animals. *Patient Patients* by artist Laura Ford include a lion with an injured paw and three monkeys: one with a cast on its leg, one with a bandaged arm and one with a sore head (www.nbt.nhs.uk).

67 Lord Mayor's Chapel

The only church of its kind in the UK

Bristol City Council is the only local authority in the UK to be responsible for the running of a church. Like muggles in the Harry Potter books unable to see the Leaky Cauldron, it is possible to walk past the Lord Mayor's Chapel without realising it is there, as it blends seamlessly in with its more modern neighbours, its tower overshadowed by office buildings.

The chapel has neither a parish nor a denomination, and is known as a 'civic peculiar'; its chaplain offers pastoral care to the lord mayor – who has a one-year term in the largely ceremonial position – and to elected councillors.

The Lord Mayor's Chapel is the sole remaining building of the 13th century Hospital of St Mark, founded by St Augustine's Abbey (the forerunner of Bristol Cathedral) and later an independent religious community which provided food for 100 poor people per day. After the dissolution of the monasteries in 1539, the hospital and its lands were purchased by the city council and were used first for Queen Elizabeth Hospital School and later for Red Maids School. In 1687, the chapel became a place of worship for Huguenots who had fled persecution in France. They used the building until 1722 when the council decided to make the chapel their official place of worship following a dispute with the cathedral.

Its nave, chancel and sanctuary date from 1230 – with the nave's ceiling particularly striking. Other aspects to look for include two beautiful side chapels, with the Jesus Chapel's floor laid with 16th-century Spanish tiles; and St Andrew's Chapel, including the effigies of two unknown knights, perhaps the founders of the original hospital. In 1822, the west window was removed from the Lord Mayor's Chapel in order to be replaced. The original window was purchased by John Cave of Brentry House and installed in a romantic Gothic folly.

Address College Green, BS1 5TB, +44 (0)117 903 1450, www.lordmayorschapel.org | Getting there At the foot of Park Street, across College Green from Bristol Cathedral | Hours Currently closed to visitors, but there is a public service at 11am every Sunday and free concerts at 1.15pm most Saturdays | Tip *Skins* fans will recognise College Green as a popular hangout from the Channel 4 drama which followed the lives of a group of unruly teenagers. Bristol Film Office has a series of online maps which plot where popular television and film productions were shot across the city (www.filmbristol.co.uk/bristol-movie-maps).

68 Metalgnu

A metal menagerie

There is a monkey holding a Rubik's Cube near Clifton Down Shopping Centre, a bull's head above the entrance to Rare butchers on North Street in Bedminster and a hawk who has caught a dove in Royal Fort Gardens (see ch. 86). These and several others scattered across Bristol and the wider area are all the creations of Julian Warren, a sculptor working under the name of Metalgnu with a keen interest in the natural world, who has also transformed his own front railings along a quiet residential street in Redland into a metal menagerie.

Warren's home is also his workshop, and the fence has become a permanent gallery and a local landmark. Among the sculptures on display at the fence are the life-sized face of a mandrill, a bird catching a fish, a crocodile hatching from an egg, and a lizard having a tug of war with an insect it has caught by its long extending tongue. The works blend in with the railing and bushes behind it; after years of exposure to the elements, the metal sculptures are almost part of the natural world themselves.

Warren studied law and archaeology at university, and worked in construction and property until the recession of the early 1990s. He first helped a friend make candlesticks out of old car parts, and with his newly found welding skills struck out on his own as a sculptor.

One of his largest sculptures in Bristol – a giant pod with a stainless-steel root growing out of it – is within the entrance lobby of Hargreaves Lansdown on Anchor Road, an 'investment supermarket' for private investors that was founded from a spare bedroom by friends Stephen Lansdown and Peter Hargreaves. The former fulfilled a boyhood dream by buying a football club, Bristol City, and later also the Bristol Bears rugby and Bristol Flyers basketball teams; the latter is one of the UK's most generous philanthropists as well as helping to bankroll the Brexit campaign.

Address 18 Burlington Road, Redland, BS6 6TL, +44 (0)117 923 8929, julianwarren@metalgnu.com, www.metalgnu.com | Getting there 2-minute walk from Whiteladies Road | Hours Unrestricted | Tip Whiteladies Road Market takes place on the corner of Whiteladies Road and Apsley Road every Saturday from 8.30am to 2pm (www.sustainableredland.org.uk).

69 Milliners' Guild

A hat for every occasion

Ani Stafford-Townsend's work has appeared on the heads of Jodie Comer in *Killing Eve* and on Aidan Turner in *Poldark*. She has helped make headdresses for *The Lion King* musical and Welsh National Opera productions, and on a top shelf in her shop and workshop is a replica of the sorting hat from the *Harry Potter* films, which she was involved in creating while on work experience early in her career.

Once upon a time we all used to wear hats. In these more secular days there is less of the need to cover our heads from God on a daily basis, unless of course you are meeting the Queen, who – at least for her most loyal subjects – is God's representative on Earth. There is still a need for hats, however, not just for garden parties at Buckingham Palace. Think weddings, trips to the races or just an excuse to dress up. When she is not busy making hats for stage and screen, Ani and her assistant Amber can make bespoke hats to order in an astonishing array of styles, from mini fascinators to wide-brimmed sunhats designed specially to fit on your head. As a former Green Party councillor in Bristol, it is no surprise that Ani has a zero-waste policy, with nothing ever getting thrown away here. During the coronavirus pandemic of 2020, she also switched from making hats to making face masks.

Although she specialises in making hats, Ani trained in costume and has recently been making a number of dresses for pantomime dames: everything from a ship costume for *Peter Pan* to a wedding-cake dress for *Aladdin*. Ani does stock the work of around a dozen other designers, but the vast majority of colourful hats packed onto the shelves are her own creations. Trans women who want to feel more feminine come to Ani to get special hats made because those on the high street are too small, and some customers are such regulars that they have unique hat shapes named after them.

Address 22 Upper Maudlin Street, BS2 8DJ, +44 (0)117 329 3003, mail@millinersguild.co.uk, www.millinersguild.co.uk | **Getting there** 2-minute walk from Christmas Steps, 5-minute walk from bus station | **Hours** Mon–Wed appointments only, Thu–Sat 10am–5pm | **Tip** Opposite the shop is a sculpture of Gromit, Wallace's canine companion in the Oscar-winning stop-motion animated films made by Aardman in Bristol. It was part of Gromit Unleashed, a trail of dozens of sculptures raising money for Bristol Children's Hospital (www.gromitunleashed.org.uk).

70__Mina Road Tunnel
An ever-changing street-art canvas

Once upon a time, a legal graffiti wall was a contradiction in terms. Painting graffiti on a wall, on private or on public property, was against the law. Stokes Croft is Bristol's best-known area for graffiti but most of it still remains officially verboten. Here's where we get into the distinction between graffiti and street art. In recent years, Bristol City Council has embraced street art as such a symbol of Bristol that City Hall has huge photographs of colourful tags in some of its staff kitchens. And much street art is now commissioned by businesses, with property developers who want to give their new developments an air of authenticity paying some of the city's best-known graffiti artists to decorate their hoardings.

There is certainly no commercial aspect to the work within the 200-foot-long Mina Road tunnel, with art along both sides and even the ceiling. The tunnel, which connects St Werburgh's with its farm (see ch. 91) underneath a railway line, changes on such a regular basis that it is futile describing what it looks like today because it will be different by tomorrow.

Walk or cycle through the tunnel and you can usually breathe in the fumes of the spray cans used by the artists hard at work, often accompanied by music whose bass reverberates along this subterranean painting space.

Mina Road tunnel has been a designated painting spot since 2008 when a team organised by the People's Republic of Stokes Croft (see ch. 96) used dozens of litres of white masonry paint as the first steps to transforming the walls. They first brushed off the flakes and laid down a good coat of masonry paint so that the space could become fit for murals. From morning to late over a weekend, the volunteers painted from the floor to the curved ceiling thanks to a few ladders and scaffolding towers, in order to create this ever-changing street-art canvas.

Address Mina Road, St Werburgh's, BS2 9YT | **Getting there** 2-minute walk from St Werburgh's City Farm; bus 5 to Victoria Street | **Hours** Unrestricted | **Tip** If a pub is owned by Dawkins, you know that you have found a good 'un. A short walk from Mina Road tunnel is the Miners Arms. Elsewhere are The Green Man and Hillgrove in Kingsdown, and The Portcullis and The Victoria in Clifton. Look out for Dawkins' beers on draught and in bottles in pubs across the city (www.dawkinsales.com).

71 Mr Langford's Plaque

Time waits for no man

Many people say that the pace of life in Bristol is slower than else-where, and it used to be officially so, with Bristol's time 10 minutes behind that in London due to the later sunrise and sunset. There is a reminder of this on the clock outside The Exchange (now St Nick's Market) on Corn Street, which has two minute hands, one ten minutes behind the other. The Greenwich Mean Time (GMT) hand is red and Bristol local time is black. This dual timekeeping became necessary with the arrival of the railways, which in Bristol saw Temple Meads originally plying the Great Western Railway and the Bristol & Exeter Railway from 1841, and the Bristol & Gloucester Railway from 1844. Trains had to run on nationwide timetables, with England adopting a standardised railway time, something that had never been attempted before.

But many people in Bristol still resisted GMT, preferring to retain the city's own time that had served them perfectly well for centuries. The city fathers only officially adopted the standard time in 1852, five years after it was established elsewhere across the rest of the country. When GMT did officially arrive in Bristol, it was received by telegraph from the Greenwich Royal Observatory in London to a clock made by William Langford. Regulated to England's new standard time, this clock sent signals to others in the city including the nearby Bristol Cathedral clock to ensure that they were all in sync.

To commemorate the job of this master clock and Langford's efforts, Bristol's smallest plaque, no larger than a 30cm ruler, can be found directly underneath the clock, now in a somewhat sorry state outside a nationwide cafe chain. Engraved on the metal plaque are the words: *This line is 2° 35' 47" west of the Greenwich Meridian (10 min. 23 secs.). In 1852, Mr Langford's electric clock took its time by telegraph from the Greenwich Royal Observatory.*

Address On the pavement outside Costa, 30 College Green, BS1 5TB | Getting there 2-minute walk from Bristol Cathedral; plenty of buses serve College Green | Hours Unrestricted | Tip Plans are currently in place to restore two Roman carved-oak soldiers, known as quarterjacks, which for more than a century hammered the quarter-hour bells on Christ Church on Broad Street. They haven't been seen or heard since 2012 when they were taken down for repainting and found to be in too poor a condition to go back outside (www.christchurchcitybristol.org/the-quarter-jacks).

72 Napier Square
A one-sided square

It is unthinkable today to imagine Queen Square in the city centre with a dual carriageway dissecting its grandeur, but that was the fate that from 1936 befell one of the largest Georgian squares in Europe when Redcliffe Way was ploughed diagonally through it – only for the road to be removed almost in time for the square's 300th anniversary in 1999. Two other fine Georgian squares, which have both seen plenty of redevelopment in recent years on the front line of Bristol's battle against gentrification, are Brunswick Square and Portland Square in St Paul's – the latter home to St Paul's Church, the headquarters of Circomedia (see ch. 37).

But there is one square in Bristol that is not a square at all. In the 1890s, there were ambitious plans for Napier Square in Avonmouth to be constructed as a grand formal public square lined on four sides with stone houses. Unfortunately, plans ground to a halt when the Great Western Railway decided to build their line to Henbury through the part-built square, similar to what Bristol Corporation did to Queen Square several decades later.

Only one side of the square exists today, squeezed against the dock boundary, with houses named after English towns such as Derby and Dover. On one end of the road is Avonmouth Village Social Club, where you can find some of the cheapest drinks in the area to accompany the karaoke.

Avonmouth celebrated its 150th anniversary in 2015, making it the same age as the Clifton Suspension Bridge. What we now know as Avonmouth did not exist before the Victorian era, prior to which the area known as River's Mouth was, according to local historian David Martyn, 'muddy, wet, exposed and inhospitable'. The modern Avonmouth grew after a new railway, still in operation today (see ch. 94), was built linking the docks in central Bristol with the tidal estuary of the River Severn.

Address Napier Square, Avonmouth, BS11 9AJ | **Getting there** Severn Beach Line from Bristol Temple Meads to Avonmouth; bus 3 to McLaren Road | **Hours** Unrestricted | **Tip** The Miles family were responsible for the development of much of Avonmouth. Have a drink in the Miles Arms pub on Avonmouth Road, and look out for an ornately carved family coat of arms high up on the Royal Hotel on Gloucester Road (www.royalhotelbristol.co.uk).

73 Nicholas Cage Pub Sign

'Put…the bunny…back…in the box'

For many years, a cardboard cut-out of Nicholas Cage looked down on passers-by from a first-floor window of the Three Tuns pub. In 2018, then-landlady Jenna Graves went one step further and gave the actor a sign outside all to himself. It portrays the Oscar-winning star of *Leaving Las Vegas* and *Con Air* as a Napoleonic-era general staring moodily into the middle distance towards Brandon Hill. We don't have any Hollywood-style walks of fame in Bristol, content on the whole to remember famous former residents with simple blue plaques. But Cage is now immortalised by this small pub on their sign, as gobby Bristol teenager Vicky Pollard from BBC comedy *Little Britain* once was on the sign of The Victoria pub in St Werburgh's.

Large figures by street artist Silent Hobo lurk on the side wall of this pub, and a forest scene by him decorates the beer garden. The pub's newest addition came about following a need to repaint the outside of the building – one of the oldest in this corner of Bristol – now in a vibrant shade of burnished orange. In addition to the fresh lick of paint, Jenna decided to put the fella from *Face/Off* on the sign, partly funded by customers buying a special pint of beer. The new sign was the crowning glory of the pub's love of the California-born actor which began with former landlord Simon Calcraft's regular Sunday hangover cure of a takeaway and watching a couple of Nicholas Cage films. Somehow, this spread into the pub and continued to spread, with photos of Cage appearing on the walls and the cardboard cut-out that used to look down onto St George's Road given to another member of staff, Laurie Dix, as a birthday present. Look closely around the Three Tuns, both inside and in the beer garden, and you might find a few more homages to Cage, who used to own a home on The Circus in Bath and turned on the city's Christmas lights in 2009.

Address The Three Tuns, 78 St George's Road, BS1 5UR | Getting there 3-minute walk
from College Green | Hours Outside unrestricted; pub open Mon & Tue 4–11pm,
Wed noon–11pm, Thu–Sat noon–midnight, Sun noon–10.30pm | Tip Dreadnought
is an independent second-hand bookshop on St George's Road specialising in the arts,
humanities and social sciences, as well as being the headquarters of Bristol Radical History
Group (www.dreadnoughtbooks.co.uk).

74__Nipper Statue

Bristol's most famous musical icon?

Face cocked to one side, Nipper is still one of the most recognisable dogs in the world, despite dying in 1895. So named because of his habit of biting the backs of visitors' legs, Nipper originally lived with his owner, Mark Henry Barraud, in the Prince's Theatre on Park Row, where Mark was a scenery designer. It is for this reason that the statue of Nipper is where it is today, located opposite what was once Bristol's biggest theatre, destroyed in a German bombing raid in 1940.

As well as a skilled craftsman, Mark was a practical joker who sent visitors to catch trout at Fishponds (where, despite its name, there is no public fishing). Nipper went everywhere with him, and when Mark died his brother Francis took care of the dog (either a Fox Terrier or a Jack Russell, nobody is certain), first living in Liverpool and later Kingston-upon-Thames. Nipper's continued fame comes from a painting Francis did of him listening intently to the voice of Mark being played from what was first a wind-up phonograph before it was changed to a gramophone. The rights to the painting – originally titled *Dog Looking at and Listening to a Phonograph* and later called *His Master's Voice* – were bought by the Gramophone Company, who changed their name to HMV after the painting, using the image as their logo ever since.

In the early noughties, Bristol street artist Banksy re-appropriated the HMV logo, giving Nipper a shoulder-mounted bazooka which he is aiming at the gramophone. The stencil, known as *Rocket Dog*, was later painted on the walls of the courtyard of Cargo nightclub in east London. In 2019, businessman Doug Putman rescued HMV shortly after it fell into administration for the second time in five years. Bristol's one remaining HMV shop is in Broadmead, where rapper Stormzy met fans at a signing session to mark the release of new album, *Heavy is the Head*, in 2020.

Address Merchant Venturers Building, 75 Woodland Road, BS8 1UB | Getting there 3-minute walk from Bristol Museum & Art Gallery | Hours Unrestricted | Tip Look out in one corner of Millennium Square for two Jack Russell terriers, Bill and Bob, swimming in a puddle. The life-size bronze sculptures were made by artist Cathie Pilkington as part of a public art commission.

75 Palestine Museum

The history of Palestine in a former nightclub

Exploring Palestinian culture, heritage and political life, the Palestine Museum & Cultural Centre was originally opened in 2013 as a 'Palestinian Embassy'. Then-lord mayor of Bristol, Faruk Choudhury, joined Manuel Hassassian, former Palestinian envoy to the UK, in conducting the opening ceremony by cutting a ceremonial green ribbon together. The museum was founded after Palestinians won 'upgraded status' at the United Nations. In the words of the museum's founders, the aim was 'to educate the ordinary people about the truth and the facts, past and present, of the Palestinian people'.

Today, the organisation is run entirely by volunteers who proudly state that they are without political affiliations and come from different backgrounds, 'of all faiths and none'. It is located within the former Arc bar and nightclub, which the Best of Bristol website remembers as 'massively grimy' and where 'you'd be offered so many drugs in there that it was like that sketch in *Brass Eye* with the made up drug names'. (Incidentally, *Brass Eye* creator Chris Morris worked as a journalist at BBC Radio Bristol before he was fired for talking over the news bulletins and making silly noises, according to his former colleague and now Radio Bristol lunchtime show presenter, Steve Yabsley.)

The Palestine Museum & Cultural Centre aims to educate, inform and communicate the story of Palestine and its people; gives a voice to the Palestinian cause; hosts events including talks, exhibitions and seminars; supports and promotes the culture and heritage of Palestine; and engages with individuals, groups and organisations in support of Palestine. Recent events have included a gig by Bethlehem-based musician Ziad Hilal, film screenings and embroidery workshops. A variety of traditional food and drink is available in Resbite Cafe on the ground floor. Try their signature oven-baked falafel.

Address 27 Broad Street, BS1 2HG, www.palmuseumbristol.org | Getting there 3-minute walk from St Nick's Market | Hours Sat & Sun 11am–6pm | Tip At the end of Broad Street is St John on the Wall church, which was built into Bristol's medieval wall in the 14th century. It acted both as part of the city's defences and a place for travellers to pray before a journey (www.visitchurches.org.uk).

76_ The Passenger Shed

A cathedral-like former railway station

When Bristol Temple Meads was first built, famous engineer Isambard Kingdom Brunel (of Clifton Suspension Bridge and SS *Great Britain* fame) designed the station building in Tudor revival style. Like the original Paddington station in London to which the railway line led, it was a terminus which consisted simply of an arrival and a departure platform. The two platforms were underneath what at the time of the station's completion in 1841 was the widest single span of its age and today remains the world's earliest surviving purpose-built passenger railway terminus.

Temple Meads was constructed outside the medieval heart of Bristol within the Temple parish. Brunel designed the station for the Great Western Railway, including a ticket office, a goods area, an engineering shop, stables for hundreds of horses and a grand boardroom which can today be hired out for meetings. Events such as trade shows, exhibitions and Christmas parties are now held in the Passenger Shed, which in its prime saw passengers pass through an undercroft holding the waiting rooms. The functional but beautiful space survives almost entirely intact and according to A. Gomme in *An Architectural History: Bristol* is 'easily the most complete survivor of the early provincial termini, and an exceptionally important one'. Look out for the cantilevered timber roof with false hammer beams above an arcade of Tudor arches on cast-iron columns. Next door, an extension to the original platforms is now used as a car park.

During its use as a railway station, locomotives were rotated on turntables and moved from line to line in what was known as the engine shed. The Exploratory science museum, the forerunner to We The Curious on Millennium Square, was housed here from 1989 to 1999, with the space later used as the Empire and Commonwealth Museum from 2002 to 2009. As the Engine Shed, it is now a thriving business hub.

Address Station Approach, BS1 6QH, +44 (0)117 922 4737,
events.thepassengershed@bristol.gov.uk, www.brunels-old-station.co.uk | Getting there
1-minute walk from Bristol Temple Meads | Hours Open during events | Tip Bristol is
fond of places with 'shed' in their name, including the marvellous M Shed museum and
the wonderful Watershed cinema and cultural powerhouse (www.watershed.co.uk).

77 Paul Dirac Memorial

Better at maths than Einstein

'God used beautiful mathematics in creating the world,' said Nobel Prize-winning scientist Paul Dirac, and his memorial on Anchor Road is an example of this beauty. Born in Bristol in 1902, Dirac has been described as the greatest mathematical physicist of the 20th century, probably second only to Albert Einstein in the originality of his work.

Dirac studied at the University of Bristol before achieving a PhD at Cambridge, later becoming Lucasian Professor of Mathematics, the position once occupied by Isaac Newton, and after Dirac by Stephen Hawking. A theoretical physicist, he has an important equation named after him (the only equation on a memorial in Westminster Abbey), was the 'inventor' of anti-matter, and his work on quantum mechanics won him the Nobel Prize for Physics in 1933.

Erected in 2000, Simon Thomas' *Small Worlds* sculpture rises 18 feet into the air in front of We The Curious, pointing towards the small worlds Dirac studied. Thomas aimed to represent colour, heat and light in the work, with these natural phenomena only described adequately by quantum theory. Made out of fibre cement, the colour of each block differs slightly from its neighbour, ranging from a cool dark magenta at the base area to a hotter and lighter sand colour at the top and centre, reminiscent of a flame. There is a commemorative plaque at Dirac's birthplace of 15 Monk Road in Bishopston, while Thomas' sculpture on Anchor Road also forms part of Engineers' Walk, a series of commemorative plaques on the side of the nearby former IMAX building, now part of Bristol Aquarium. Remembered here are famous names such as Isambard Kingdom Brunel, as well as less famous ones including hot air balloon innovator Don Cameron; Ralph Benjamin, inventor of the computer mouse; and Brunel protégé Charles Richardson, a railway engineer who also invented the spliced cricket bat.

Address Anchor Road, BS1 5DB | **Getting there** 1-minute walk from Millennium Square | **Hours** Unrestricted | **Tip** The Shy Fountain on the opposite side of Anchor Road to College Square only exists when no one is there. The playful site-specific work by artist Simon Faithfull disappears like a startled animal whenever somebody approaches. Try and coax it back to life by staying completely still.

78 Pipe Walk

Water everywhere; no longer a drop to drink

For many years, the only supply of clean, fresh water for the people of Redcliffe came from a pipe running from Knowle's Northern Slopes, the well head now well-hidden in the middle of some allotments. The 800-year-old pipe ended at St Mary Redcliffe Church, with parishioners regularly walking the two-mile route of the pipe to check for any anomalies. Originally made of lead but replaced with cast iron in the 19th century, it has not supplied water since being damaged during World War II, but churchgoers still take part in an annual 'pipe walk' from its start to its finish, with periodic stops made for inspections of the pipe. The meander takes in Victoria Park in south Bristol, where first-time pipe walkers, including clergy as well as parishioners, are traditionally held aloft above one of several old stone markers indicating the route and bearing the inscription 'S.M.R. Pipe'.

Also in Victoria Park is a water maze made out of bricks by Jane Norbury and Peter Milner, whose design replicates one of the medieval roof bosses in St Mary Redcliffe. Commissioned by the former Avon County Council and Wessex Water, it was built in 1984 at the point where the pipe is crossed by a 20th-century sewer and storm drain. Sadly, spring water carried here along the pipe from Knowle no longer flows from a central sluice all around the brick channels of the maze.

Known as a 'Chartres maze' after the labyrinth with no end set into the floor of the nave of Chartres Cathedral in France, the water maze is a relatively new feature in Victoria Park. Many of the original features of the park – which as its name suggests was first laid out in Victorian times – such as a bandstand and swimming pool have long gone. But it still has colourful flowerbeds, a rock garden, wildlife area and popular playground, as well as one of the best panoramic views over Bristol from anywhere in the city.

ST. MARY REDCLIFFE MAZE

This maze commemorates the recognition of the need for clean water

Address Victoria Park, BS3 (maze closest to Hill Avenue side) | Getting there 10-minute walk from Bristol Temple Meads; bus 91 to St John's Lane | Hours Unrestricted | Tip Jamia Mosque on Green Street in Totterdown, a 7-minute walk away, was converted from an Anglican church, becoming Bristol's first mosque in 1968. Its dome and minaret were added in 1980.

79 Prince Rupert's Gate

A reminder of Bristol's role in the English Civil War

Bristol was twice besieged during the Civil War – the last major active military campaign on English soil – and even though it ended more than 350 years ago, its reminders are still surprisingly plentiful. A gatehouse which once formed part of a Royalist bastion is now used as a meeting room by the University of Bristol, while stone fortifications almost obscured by vegetation at the foot of Brandon Hill are all that survive of the Water Fort, the only known substantial upstanding remains of Bristol's Civil War outer defensive ring.

Prince Rupert's Gate was originally built as an entrance to what was known as Windmill Hill Fort, which was renamed Royal Fort when taken by the Royalists in 1643. The Royalists held Bristol for two years. Then in 1645, Lord Fairfax and Oliver Cromwell appeared on the scene and regained the city after a 20-day siege. The taking of the Royal Fort has been described as 'a very gentlemanly skirmish' with the fort itself barely seeing any real action. One theory as to why Rupert conceded so easily was that the structure was still not fully completed, nor the water supply abundant enough to sustain his troops. In 1655, Cromwell ordered the fort's demolition and today Prince Rupert's Gate is the only surviving part. Until recently, the gatehouse was used for small-group teaching, primarily by the University of Bristol maths department. Now that the mathematicians have moved elsewhere, the gatehouse has been reallocated to Student Services.

During the Civil War, earth ramparts linked Fremantle Square in Kingsdown, where the 13-gun Prior's Hill Fort once occupied a crucial high position, with the Royal Fort. You can visit the spot by making the steep walk up Ninetree Hill from Stokes Croft. The name Kingsdown comes from the Middle Ages, when this area was used to exercise the King's horses for the Royal Garrison of Bristol.

Address Royal Fort Road, Kingsdown, BS2 8DH | **Getting there** Bus 9 or 72 to St Michael's Hill | **Hours** Unrestricted | **Tip** The Wills Memorial Building is a Bristol landmark on top of Park Street. Built in 1925, it houses the University of Bristol's earth sciences and law departments as well as the great hall which hosts graduation ceremonies and public events. Tours up the tower raise money for Wallace & Gromit's Grand Appeal (www.bristol.ac.uk/university/visit/tower-tours).

80_ Psychopomp

A distillery disguised as a greengrocer's

If you ask Psychopomp's Danny Walker when his distillery began, you get two answers. Officially, gin was first distilled at these premises on St Michael's Hill in 2013. Unofficially, production started several years earlier as Danny began to perfect his craft in the basement of his co-founder Liam Hirt's home in Montpelier. Woden, the pair's first gin – a classic London dry with juniper berries, coriander seed, angelica root, cassia bark, fresh grapefruit zest and fennel seed – is still made all year round. Seasonal varieties, named after Norse gods, are produced for two years before being replaced by a new recipe. During the 2020 pandemic, the team used gin botanicals to make hand sanitiser, and livestreamed cocktail-making masterclasses.

From the outside, Psychopomp has the appearance of an old greengrocers, with the original hand-painted sign advertising A. Jenkins' groceries and provisions still in situ. At one end of the room are the copper pot stills. The finished liquids (gin, absinthe, aquavit, coffee digestifs) sit on shelves next to glass jars of botanicals for future recipes. This is very much a working distillery with a bar offering perfect cocktails attached. When not serving, Danny and the team tend to the distilling process. Drip by drip, a new drink is created in front of your eyes.

Like the seasonal gins, there are seasonal 'distiller's table' events here with drinks created around themes such as Bonfire Night or Christmas. You can even have a go at distilling, leaving with a bottle of your own recipe. While gin can be produced within hours, it takes much longer to make a whisky, with the law stipulating that it must be matured in oak casks for a minimum of three years. Psychopomp's sister distillery, Circumstance in Whitehall, is due to have whisky ready by late-2021. It will be the first whisky produced in Bristol for a generation.

Address 145 St Michael's Hill, Kingsdown, BS2 8DB, +44 (0)7511 934675, info@microdistillery.co.uk, www.microsdistillery.co.uk | Getting there 15-minute walk from Stokes Croft; bus 9 or 72 to St Michael's Hill | Hours Wed–Sat noon–10pm | Tip Bristol Distilling Co. was founded in 2018 by the same team behind steak and burger restaurant Chomp on St Nicholas Street (www.chompgrill.co.uk). Specialising in flavoured gins, their distillery in Bedminster also has a bar (www.bristoldistilling.com).

81 Quakers' Burial Ground

A hermit, lead shot and a runaway car

Once known as the Redrock Garden after the colour of the rocks in this area, what is still known as the Quakers' Burial Ground (although no burials have taken place here for almost a century) was purchased by the Quakers in 1665 to use as a cemetery. The garden today includes raised beds and a cherry tree that was planted in 1998 to mark the life of Christopher Merrick, a former president of Bristol's Junior Chamber of Commerce, with a plaque remembering that he *died here whilst averting his runaway car, to save the lives of others*. Ford recalled all its Explorer vehicles for checks following his death.

Hundreds of Quakers were buried here until it ceased being a cemetery in 1923, with headstones revealing the youngest to die was only eight months old and the oldest was 99. Dozens of the headstones are now stacked in another unusual feature of this small park, a hermitage, which is a Scheduled Ancient Monument. The hermit's cave, also known as St John's hermitage, was the home from 1346 of John Sparkes, who was installed here by Thomas, Lord Berkeley to pray for him and his family. Successive hermits continued to occupy the cave until the 17th century.

Until the 1960s there were shops and houses along this side of Redcliffe Hill, with the Quakers' Burial Ground hidden behind them. These included one home with the unusual addition of a tower built onto its roof in 1782 by plumber William Watts. By dropping molten lead from the tower into a deep well below, Watts could create perfectly spherical lead shot, an invention that made his fortune. He sold his business for £10,000, a huge sum at the time, and invested it in speculative property development. Sadly, Windsor Terrace in Clifton overlooking the Avon Gorge was originally known as Watts' Folly, as he spent all his money before the foundations were complete, going bankrupt in 1794.

Address Redcliffe Way, Redcliffe, BS1 6SJ | Getting there 1-minute walk from St Mary Redcliffe church, 3-minute walk from Queen Square | Hours Unrestricted | Tip Walk through Redcliffe Wharf to find the historic Ostrich pub overlooking the Floating Harbour, with one of Bristol's best outside seating areas. It reopened in 2020 with a new first-floor dining room and bar (www.theostrichbristol.co.uk).

82 Recession
Retro clothes, records, repartee and more

It's difficult to adequately describe Recession, a small shop at the foot of Jacob's Wells Road backing onto Brandon Hill. The only way to truly understand its charms is to pay a visit and strike up conversation with its one-of-a-kind proprietor, Gill Loats. You may well find her sitting on a leopard-print throne with gold skulls on the armrests, which was made for her 60th birthday party. She is a shopkeeper, author, fashion show impresario, pantomime director and expert on Bristol's female music scene. Her next book will be about The Dug Out, the club where Massive Attack made their name while still the Wild Bunch collective, and where Gill became the first woman DJ after talking herself behind the decks.

In many ways, Recession, which was opened at the peak of the recession in 2008, encapsulates Gill's varied life, which started when her adoptive parents moved from London to Bristol soon after she was born. It is quirky, fun and individual, stocking clothes from the 1920s to the 1980s, as well as what Gill calls her 'bits and bobs' – which at any given time might include everything from records to books, buttons to bookmarks. Gill is not one for minimalism and collects items like a magpie. The shop grew from her own collection she still keeps at home as well as regular trips to auctions and charity shops. Calling it an Aladdin's cave would be to undersell its wonder.

Twice a year, Gill hosts a fashion show at the Southbank Club in Southville, where many of the clothes from the shop are worn and then sold, leading to the next restocking of Recession's rails. 2020 saw the 20th such show, whose recent themes have included space and cruising. Her personal favourite era is the 1970s, and she always has, as she says, a good stock of 1970s' 'kitsch'. Items range in price from three to several hundred pounds, with Gill's repartee thrown in for free.

Address 8 Jacob's Wells Road, Hotwells, BS8 1EA, recessiongill@gmail.com, www.instagram.com/recessiongill | **Getting there** 5-minute walk from College Green | **Hours** Thu–Sat noon–5pm(ish) | **Tip** Walk up the White Hart Steps from Jacob's Wells Road roundabout up to the colourful houses of Cliftonwood, looking out for hot air balloon mosaics on the way. The entrance passes underneath St Peter's House, named after the late-19th-century church which stood here until 1939.

83 __ Redland Standing Stone
A mysterious monolith

People sit on it, walk past it, ignore it. How did it get to its position near the Hartington Park and Woodstock Road junction in the south-eastern corner of Redland Green? Nobody actually knows. One theory is that it is a sarsen stone – these are blocks of sandstone intentionally placed in a pattern of which Stonehenge in Wiltshire is the most famous example in England. There were reputedly at least two stone circles in this area of Bristol, and this particular stone may be all that now remains. If so, where did it come from, and where on Earth are its mates?

Another theory is that the stone is the last remains of an ancient burial chamber or perhaps some other marker stone. Its journey to get here may be unknown, but it most definitely is a stone of great antiquity, dating back to before the arrival of the Romans, putting paid to a third theory that it was placed here next to the presumed line of the Roman road from Bath to Sea Mills (the largest settlement in the Bristol area at that time) as a shrine where offerings could be given for safe travel.

There were once more isolated stones like this scattered around Bristol, with another in the gardens of a house in Armoury Square in Easton – which once had a companion stone nearby. Fans of mysterious rocks should also head to Woodland Road, where just a (much smaller) stone's throw from the statue of Nipper (see ch. 74) there is a huge block of sandstone on display. Unlike the Redland standing stone, we know the story of how it got to its current location. A plaque in front of it reveals that it is one of two large nodules of sandstone found in 1837 during the excavation of a railway tunnel in St Anne's and preserved by Isambard Kingdom Brunel himself. It was presented to the University of Bristol by British Rail in 1983 and now sits on a small patch of grass opposite the rear of the Wills Memorial Building.

Address Woodstock Road, Redland, BS6 7HE | Getting there 10-minute walk from Whiteladies Road | Hours Unrestricted | Tip Regarded by many as one of Bristol's finest Georgian buildings, Redland Parish Church was built in 1743 as a private chapel for the Cossins family of nearby Redland Court. Unusually, the church is not dedicated to a saint due to an ecclesiastical dispute soon after it opened (www.redland.org.uk).

84 River Frome
Bristol's lost river

Beneath the streets of Bristol flows a river. At the peak of the city's prosperity, when Bristol was England's second most important port after London, a forest of masts used to come right into the middle of the city along this river, the Frome (it rhymes with 'zoom'), with merchant ships arriving packed with goods from all over the world. When the statue of slave trader Edward Colston was toppled from its plinth in 2020, it was thrown into the former course of the Frome next to Pero's Bridge, fittingly named after a slave.

Until the mid-19th century, the Frome was open along its whole length and crossed by a dozen bridges in Bristol alone. Now mostly covered over, only a short stretch of the river remains in the city centre, forming part of the Floating Harbour, from the Arnolfini to the Cascade Steps. It then disappears below ground until close to Cabot Circus car park, from where its journey continues through St Paul's, under the M32 motorway and beyond to its source in a quiet Gloucestershire field.

The Frome gets its name from the Anglo-Saxon word 'frum', which means rapid and vigorous. Bristol was built where the Frome meets the Avon. Both rivers once fed the moat of Bristol Castle (see ch. 19), with surrounding marshes drained over the centuries and the growing city built on top.

For many people living in east Bristol, the Frome is known by its nickname of the 'Danny'. This could be because the Victorian popularity of Johann Strauss' *Blue Danube Waltz* led to the tongue-in-cheek comparison of the Frome to the Danube, shortened to Danny. Another theory is that the name comes from the Australian word 'dunny', meaning outside toilet, with the Frome at some points in its history resembling an open sewer. A third theory is that it was named after 'Danny Boy', a song once sung by a mother as a lament for her son who drowned in the river while fishing.

Address City centre section starts close to No. 1 Harbourside, 1 Canon's Road, BS1 5UH; St Jude's section starts close to the Salvation Army's Logos House, Wade Street, St Jude's, BS2 9EL | **Getting there** City centre section 1-minute walk from Watershed; St Jude's section 2-minute walk from Cabot Circus | **Hours** Unrestricted | **Tip** St Mary-on-the-Quay church was built in 1839 facing Bristol's docks on the original line of the River Frome. Now several hundred yards from the water, it was constructed for the short-lived Irvingites (the Catholic Apostolic Church) but soon purchased by the Roman Catholics (www.stmaryonthequay.com).

85   Room 212

At the heart of Bristol's art scene

Both a shop and a gallery showcasing the work of Bristol creatives, Room 212 is a perfect introduction to some of the city's best artists, and in particular the thriving arts scene around Gloucester Road. It's certainly a building that is impossible to miss, with regularly changing window displays and a stencil of actor Cary Grant (who grew up as plain Archibald Leach just a few hundred yards away) by street artist Stewy. Behind the till there might be owner Sarah Thorp, herself an artist, or one of the other artists whose work is for sale.

Banners on lampposts the length of Gloucester Road display the handiwork of many of the artists on display and for sale here, stretching from the Memorial Stadium to the arches. Sarah says that she had a tear in her eye when this project that she had been planning for several years came to fruition. One of the busiest people in Bristol, she also has an eco-house in the back garden of the shop; offers high quality prints for artists, photographers and illustrators through 212 Productions; and used to own Alchemy 198 – a cafe, bar and gallery hosting live music, workshops and comedy nights just a few doors down from the shop – which was due to reopen as Bottles & Books bar in September 2020. She has also taken Room 212 on the road to the Green Man festival in the Brecon Beacons, with a pop-up shop in a yurt where she offered workshops inspired by nature.

After arriving in Bristol from Tobago, Sarah threw herself into the city's artistic community, helping to organise arts trails and then bringing many of her contacts together under one roof. The aim of Room 212, which opened in 2013, was to provide a local hub for artists. It has the feel of a permanent art trail, with around 100 artists featured, their familiar and not-so-familiar scenes of Bristol making perfect gifts. Sarah also hopes that everybody can be inspired by the original and creative work of others.

Address 212 Gloucester Road, Bishopston, BS7 8NU, +44 (0)7702 598090, newtwist@mail.com, www.room212.co.uk | Getting there Bus 72, 73, 75 or 76 to Gloucester Road | Hours Mon–Sat 9am–6pm | Tip Among the plethora of good places to eat and drink on Gloucester Road, one of the best is Fed 303. Try their breakfast brioche bun, sourdough toasties or caramel blondie (www.fedcafe.co.uk).

86 Royal Fort Garden

A jewel in the heart of the University

Seventy-six vertical polished steel plates form *Follow Me*, a sculpture by Jeppe Hein which was commissioned as part of the University of Bristol's centenary celebrations in 2009. Step inside to experience the disorientating effect of multiple reflections. In the creation of the piece, Hein was inspired by the early-19th-century history of the gardens, which had the effect of an uninterrupted landscape rolling down to the river. There were pathways hidden below retaining walls, and trees and scrub softening the view of the city and screening the 'unsightly rows of houses'. Elsewhere within the gardens, another public artwork, *Hollow* by Katie Paterson, is made from tree samples from across the world. Crouch down to squeeze inside and find yourself within a world of more than 10,000 unique tree specimens spanning millions of years.

Wrought-iron gates and stone pillars at the main entrance to the gardens are from a time when its driveway swept uninterrupted from this point through open parklands to Queen's Road. Another entrance is Prince Rupert's Gate (see ch. 79). The gardens originally surrounded Royal Fort House, built between 1758 and 1762 for Thomas Tyndall, a wealthy merchant. Its three facades in three different classical styles were a compromise after three separate architects had submitted designs. Nearby, there is the incongruous site of the ornamental Ivy Gate, retained as a remnant of Tyndall's formal garden estate but now marooned next to a fortunately temporary collection of Portakabins.

The other major building here is the H. H. Wills Physics Laboratory, a Gothic-style building designed by Sir George Oatley, who also designed other prominent structures including the Wills Memorial Building. The laboratory was meant to be part of a series of buildings which if constructed would have destroyed much of Royal Fort Garden under their foundations.

Address Tyndall Avenue, Kingsdown, BS8 1UH, www.bristol.ac.uk/external-estate |
Getting there Short walk from the Clifton Triangle, or bus 9 to Tyndall Avenue |
Hours Unrestricted | Tip The nearby Cloakroom Cafe opened in 2019 in a 115-year-old former Edwardian toilet block on Woodland Road. Many of the original features have been maintained in this splendid Grade II-listed building (www.instagram.com/thecloakroom_cafe).

87 St Bartholomew's Hospital
Ships and skeletons on a Saxon site

On a plinth just inside the stone archway leading to what used to be St Bartholomew's Hospital is a decapitated statue of the Virgin Mary and baby Jesus that might have been an original feature of the hospital founded here in the 13th century. The statue's feet have been rubbed smooth, perhaps for good luck by those entering the hospital centuries ago.

Located on what was once a bank of the River Frome (see ch. 84), the site of St Bartholomew's Hospital has been occupied since the late Saxon era, with the earliest archaeological finds here including boat nails dating back to the 12th century and skeletons from over the following centuries. Over time, it has been a grand house, a hospital and a monastery. It closed shortly before the Dissolution of the Monasteries in 1532, when Bristol Grammar School was established on the site. After 1847, it was adapted as housing and a printer's premises, with some elements of the former Norman hall and the hospital church, as well as substantial parts of the 18th- and 19th-century school buildings, skilfully incorporated into a 1984 office building. This was later converted into flats.

An in-depth study by archaeologists excavating the site prior to its early 1980s' redevelopment reported that 'in comparison with other Bristol hospitals, St Bartholomew's seems to have been fairly well esteemed by the citizens, but it was always bedevilled by lack of funds. It was a small-scale, fairly typical hospital of its time.' To its rear is a vertical cliff rising 70 metres high that was formed by the Frome in the same manner as the Avon Gorge, with the original hospital squeezed between the cliff face and the water's edge. Walk along Johnny Ball Lane (named after medieval merchant John a Ball, not the Bristol-born children's television presenter popular in the 1970s and 1980s) to experience part of this geology dating back to the Ice Age.

Address Christmas Street, BS1 5BT | **Getting there** 1-minute walk from Christmas Steps | **Hours** Unrestricted (but private) | **Tip** Hotel Du Vin on Narrow Lewins Mead is inside the last relic of Bristol's sugar industry, with a sugar refinery first established here in 1728. A 19th-century engine-house chimney is now part of the hotel's reception (www.hotelduvin.com/bristol).

88 St Edith's Well

Only recently rediscovered

Stourhead in Wiltshire has a lot to answer for. Not simply content to be the home – or hopefully just the present custodian – of Bristol's original High Cross (see ch. 57), it is where the medieval St Edith's Well monument is also located. The fate of the ornate gothic structure, known as a castelette and put in place to prevent contamination, was sealed when it became a hindrance to the narrow streets that once made up the area that today is Castle Park. It was taken down in 1733 before being installed at Stourhead three decades later.

St Edith's Well was one of Bristol's oldest sources of drinking water and may have been crucial in the development of the early Saxon town of Brigstowe. First recorded in the late-14th century, its story was brought up to date in 2019 when the well shaft – only rediscovered in 1992 during re-landscaping of Castle Park – was repointed and topped with a reinforced glass panel. The well once supplied the people of the town and also St Peter's Hospital (an ornate building completely destroyed in the Blitz) in its role as a poor house, with contemporary accounts commenting that the water was 'remarkable for its constancy and bright sparkling appearance'.

While today you can stand on top of the well shaft, before 2019 the well had been sealed beneath flagstones and forgotten. But the area around it had begun to subside, with archaeologists commissioned to carry out a survey of the structure during restoration works, which also saw the construction of permanent picnic tables close to the kiosk containing Edna's Kitchen, famous for its falafels. The Duke of Kent officially inaugurated the newly restored well, which also received a blessing from the Bishop of Bristol, Viv Faull. The duke then made the short journey to another corner of Castle Park to open a new memorial garden honouring Sikh soldiers who lost their lives in the World Wars.

Address St Peter's Square, Castle Park, BS1 3XD | Getting there 3-minute walk from St Nick's Market | Hours Unrestricted | Tip Around one side of St Peter's Church is the Castle Park Physic Garden. A previously neglected sensory and herb garden was in 2015 transformed by perfumery Jo Malone, funded by charity sales of a scented candle, and is now cared for by volunteers from St Mungo's homeless charity (www.mungos.org).

ST EDITH'S
WELL

89__St Mary le Port

Fans of abandoned spaces? This one's for you!

Viewed from Corn Street, St Mary le Port's tower just pokes up over the top of the former Bank of England building. Look back from Castle Park and the tower stands in the middle of two others behind it, St Nicholas Church to the left and Christ Church with St Ewin to the right – a reminder of just how close the rest of the centre of Bristol came to disaster when St Mary le Port was among the hundreds of buildings destroyed during bombing raids in November 1940. One of Bristol's oldest buildings now lies forgotten and neglected behind ugly post-war concrete, with successive plans to revitalise this corner of Castle Park coming and going.

The original line of St Mary Le Port Street, an important thoroughfare which once passed next to the church, is still preserved, coming out directly opposite the High Street entrance to St Nick's Market. Houses along the road overhung so far that neighbours living on opposite sides were able to shake hands out of their windows. But it now ends in a rusty metal gate, padlocked shut and with barbed wire on top.

Walk by the concrete pyramid (see ch. 31), past some planters left behind by Extinction Rebellion protesters who closed nearby Bristol Bridge to cars for a few days in 2019 by putting a bright pink boat in the middle of it, and through a small car park used by St Nick's stallholders, and you will come to some steps leading to the sad remains of St Mary le Port.

Excavations in the 1960s revealed that the church had late Saxon or early Norman origins; its 15th-century name indicated a proximity to the market. The 15th-century tower is fenced off, with ivy climbing almost half its height on one corner. A few stunted walls, now mostly rubble, remain to be explored, with a couple of trees growing where the congregation once sat in their pews and a 16th-century domestic cellar beneath a metal grill.

Address Castle Park, BS1 2AN | Getting there 2-minute walk from St Nick's Market | Hours Unrestricted | Tip The bombed-out remains of St Peter's Church in the middle of Castle Park are a memorial to Bristol's civilian war dead. Plaques on one wall underneath the tower list their names.

90 St Philip's Footbridge
The £3m bridge to nowhere

When the annals of Bristol in the first few decades of the new millennium come to be written, the saga of the city's arena will feature strongly. An arena was first proposed in Bristol (the only major UK city not to have one) in 2003 on two hectares of land next to Temple Meads that soon became known as Arena Island. The city council purchased the land in 2004 for £15m, with an arena expected to be open by 2008 to coincide with Bristol's bid to be named European Capital of Culture. But work never started. Land at Ashton Vale was briefly set to be the site for the arena before the attention returned to Arena Island. Funding was approved, architects appointed, planning permission granted and operators announced. And then architect-turned-independent-mayor George Ferguson ceded the reins of the city to Labour's Marvin Rees, and the Arena Island arena was scrapped, with planning permission granted in 2020 for an arena in Filton in north Bristol.

Plans are now in place for 500 homes, a hotel, conference centre and office blocks for Arena Island, now known as Temple Island. But reminders of what might have been remain, in particular St Philip's footbridge, which was meant to carry concertgoers to the arena but is now a bridge to nowhere.

With Temple Island still an empty patch of land, you can cross the £3m bridge – now blighted by tagging – over the River Avon, but, once there, you can proceed no further than a metal cage. The 50-metre-long, four-metre-wide forked bridge is an impressive piece of engineering, designed to accommodate the significant height difference between the two riverbanks. 'A holistic architectural, functional and structural approach results in a bridge that is compact and clearly legible for users while being architecturally distinctive,' say Knight Architects. For now, it is its own destination. It's just a shame it goes nowhere.

Address River Avon Path, St Philip's Marsh, BS2 0XA | Getting there 7-minute walk from Bristol Temple Meads | Hours Unrestricted | Tip Bristol Animal Rescue Centre on Albert Road has been helping animals of all shapes and sizes since 1887. As well as a re-homing centre that has been used by Bristol-born actor Maisie Williams, there is also a 24-hour veterinary clinic for injured animals (www.bristolarc.org.uk).

91 St Werburgh's City Farm

Pigs in the city

There was a new kid on the block during a recent visit to St Werburgh's City Farm. She was the daughter (or perhaps the son, it was hard to tell) of Barley and Acorn, the farm's resident goats. In the pen next door was a woolly animal lying down. 'I thought that was just hay,' one 20-something said to his friends. 'But it's a sheep!' We are city dwellers in Bristol but a trip here is an opportunity temporarily to be country folk, even if we don't all leave as experts.

The farm was built in 1980 on derelict land, with a recent extension used as a base for volunteers and to host education projects. The small, two-acre site is free to enter and backs onto allotments, with sheds of all shapes and sizes marking territory. The farm has its own polytunnel here, which offers training opportunities for disadvantaged members of the local community, creating a crucial avenue of funds by growing and selling plants.

As well as the goats and sheep, there are usually chickens, ducks, pigs and rabbits, and turkeys before Christmas. This is not an animal sanctuary, so some of these animals do end up as food. A small shed close to the entrance has been converted into a shop where you can buy everything from apple-and-courgette chutney to goat's milk soap. You pay by placing money in an honesty box, with all profits going to support the farm's work.

Just the other side of the road from the farm is a cafe that looks as if it should belong in a Salvador Dalí painting. Also bringing to mind Hobbiton in *The Lord of the Rings*, the building feels as if it has been carved from the inside of a giant tree. The farm provides many of the ingredients on the menu, with allotment holders also encouraged to trade their surplus in return for something to eat or drink. The cafe's decking overlooks a small playground perfect for little ones to let off steam, with the Farm pub on the other side of the fence blessed with one of Bristol's best beer gardens.

Address Watercress Road, St Werburgh's, BS2 9YJ, +44 (0)117 942 8241, office@swcityfarm.co.uk, www.swcityfarm.co.uk | **Getting there** Bus 5 to James Street and walk down Mina Road | **Hours** Daily 9am–4pm | **Tip** Popti & Beast on Mina Road is a fabulous collaboration between a butcher and a baker. Buy meat sourced from ethically minded farms in Devon and Somerset as well as breads, sweet treats and savoury snacks all baked on the premises (www.poptiandbeast.co.uk).

92 — Sea Mills Museum

A memorable use for an old telephone box

As part of a heritage project celebrating 100 years of the Sea Mills estate, a disused red telephone box was transformed into one of the UK's smallest museums. One of its first displays marked Remembrance Sunday, including the story of an 18-year-old, among the first people to be born in Sea Mills, who died on a convoy ship during World War II. Also remembered are an American soldier billeted here, and a Jewish family who escaped the Nazis and found safety in nearby Sylvan Way.

A decorated Christmas tree inside the telephone box was an early indication that something unusual was afoot. Work started to restore it in February 2019, with a lamp and lampshade installed as part of Window Wanderland, an art project which usually sees front windows rather than telephone boxes brightly decorated. With a lick of paint, new signage and a floor made from old coins, the first display included oral history recordings and a related heritage trail across Sea Mills which saw current homeowners researching former residents of their house.

Overlooking the telephone box is Addison's Oak, which in 2019 was shortlisted in the Woodland Trust's Tree of the Year competition. Described as 'one of Bristol's most important monuments', it was planted in 1919 to mark the start of the building of a citywide public housing scheme that was to provide 'homes fit for heroes' returning from World War I. The mini museum is located within what is officially a K6 kiosk, designed by Sir Giles Gilbert Scott to commemorate the silver jubilee of King George V in 1935. Scott was also an architect, who in Bristol designed Electricity House, now luxury flats in the city centre, and 37-39 Corn Street, originally a bank and now student accommodation. There were some 60,000 examples of the K6 installed across the British Isles, but only this one in Sea Mills is believed to be used in such a way.

Address Junction of Shirehampton Road and St Edyth's Road, Sea Mills, BS9 2DY, www.seamills100.co.uk | Getting there Severn Beach railway line to Sea Mills; bus 4 to Sea Mills Square | Hours Sun–Fri 9am–5pm, Sat 10am–5pm | Tip Another old building with a new use in Sea Mills is Café on the Square, a cafe within a former public toilet (www.cafeonthesquare.org.uk).

93 — Seven Saints of St Paul's

Honouring seven esteemed legacies

After a four-year project remembering the origins of St Paul's Carnival in time for its 50th anniversary celebrations in 2018, which also coincided with the 70th anniversary of the arrival of the Windrush generation, the incredible stories of seven people were represented on huge murals across their own neighbourhood of Bristol. Alongside their faces, known to so many, are symbols and quotes representing their tireless work in the community. These colourful, poignant murals created by artist Michele Curtis celebrate *The Seven Saints of St Paul's*: Audley Evans, Barbara Dettering, Carmen Beckford, Clifford Drummond, Delores Campbell, Owen Henry and Roy Hackett.

Michele worked closely with the surviving members of the seven to best represent their stories, and was told plenty of tales by family members of those who had died, which allowed her to honour their legacies. The idea for the project came to Michele while she was still a student at City of Bristol College, but she never thought that her charcoal and graphite portraits on paper would just a few years later be transformed on such a large scale, with a one-off exhibition becoming a permanent heritage trail and outdoor gallery, accompanied by a mobile app. Michele says that she uses art as a platform to share the experiences of the African Caribbean community in Bristol, for whom St Paul's Carnival is much more than just a street party; it's a celebration of their heritage. The carnival founders were all members of the Bristol West Indian Parents & Friends Association, which was also the organisation behind the Bristol Bus Boycott (see ch. 18). As well as honouring the work of the seven, Michele hopes that the project will have a wider influence on the subject of cultural diversity in Bristol, saying, 'Our identity as British citizens is a shared identity and a melting pot of many different cultures.'

Address Various locations, www.iconicblackbritons.com/the-seven-saints-of-stpauls | Getting there Bus 5 to City Road | Hours Unrestricted | Tip St Paul's Adventure Playground has for many years been a popular hangout. The community rallied around the playground in order to rebuild it following an arson attack in 2020 (www.apeproject.co.uk).

94 Severn Beach Line

Escape to the country

Don't catch the Severn Beach Line if you are expecting to walk across white sand to dip your toes into an azure blue sea. Severn Beach is more muddy than Mediterranean, but if you want an easy way to get between the city centre and Bristol's western suburbs without getting stuck in traffic, this is the railway line for you. 'You can get from anywhere in Bristol to anywhere in Bristol on the Severn Beach Line,' said comedian Riordan DJ in livestreamed charity comedy show Belly Laughs during the 2020 lockdown. 'Apart from a large chunk of Bristol.'

Ride the Severn Beach Line enough and the stops will be ingrained in your brain like tracks from a favourite album: Lawrence Hill, Stapleton Road, Montpelier, Redland, Clifton Down, Sea Mills, Shirehampton, Avonmouth, St Andrew's Road and Severn Beach. Look out for ghost signs on nearby buildings as the train pulls into Lawrence Hill, enjoy a panoramic view of St Werburgh's, and then after Clifton Down a tunnel brings you out into countryside still well within the city boundaries. At Avonmouth, the train heads close to the docks where Prime Minister Boris Johnson visited before the 2019 general election. He should have taken the Severn Beach Line back to Bristol city centre, because he got stuck in traffic on the way to his next appointment.

The Severn Beach Line is a line to be celebrated, with Friends of Suburban Bristol Railways campaigning successfully to increase the frequency of its services and Severnside Community Rail Partnership funding improvements to stations, including street artist Silent Hobo working with local schoolchildren to add new murals to the walls of Montpelier. For the Food Connections festival in 2018, there was even afternoon tea organised for passengers. If you do get to Severn Beach, check out the Just As You Are Tea Cottage. But leave your bucket and spade at home.

Address Starts at Bristol Temple Meads, BS1 6QF, and finishes at Severn Beach, BS35 4PL, www.discoversevernbeachline.co.uk | **Getting there** Get on at any of the 11 stations along the line | **Hours** Check timetables | **Tip** Get off at Stapleton Road in Easton to explore one of Bristol's most cosmopolitan and vibrant areas. Once unfairly disparaged in a tabloid newspaper as 'Britain's most dangerous road', it is now home to an amazing array of independent businesses.

95 — South Bristol Berry Maze
Forage for free in the city

'Feel free to roam and pick up berries', reads a sign at the berry maze next to the Malago Greenway cycle path, 'this is a project for the community, by the community!' A roam here turns a visitor into a forager and is free throughout the year, with children able to enjoy the space to play in while their adults think about which would be the best berries to pick for a crumble or a jam.

The berry maze is the first of its kind in the UK and was created in 2017 out of the desire for a natural community hub which local residents could use, forage in and enjoy. The initial design was created by nine-year-old Harry Ward, a pupil from nearby Parson Street Primary School, with local businesses donating money. Dozens of volunteers got involved in litter-picking events as the maze took shape on land that was previously overgrown with weeds, overrun with litter and plagued with dog mess.

The maze (although it's a stretch to call it that when not in full bloom) now features more than 250 plants and 17 varieties of edible berries, 'from the humble blackberry to the exciting jostaberry' according to that sign. Don't know what a jostaberry is? Well, its ancestry includes blackcurrant, gooseberry and a species of wild gooseberry; its fruit is very similar to a blackcurrant in appearance but is about twice the size with a sweet gooseberry-like flavour; and its bush is thornless and heavy-yielding. You will certainly leave the maze after your visit knowing more about berries than you did before.

Two years after it first opened, a grant from the National Lottery Awards for All is enabling a new project to be installed in the centre of the maze. The new installation will feature a three-dimensional replica of Harry's initial map and also include giant flowers and insects, all crafted from rubbish and recycled materials found in the wasteland on which the maze was created.

Address Between Lynton Road and Brixham Road, Bedminster, BS3 5LL,
www.facebook.com/TheBerryMaze2017 | Getting there Walk or cycle along the Malago
Greenway path connecting Hartcliffe, Hengrove and Bedminster with the city centre;
bus 511 to Lynton Road | Hours Unrestricted | Tip No gym? No problem. Run or walk up
and down the almost 200 Novers Steps, which start the other side of Lynton Road from
the maze, taking you from Bedminster to Knowle West. Climb them 246 times to reach the
height of Mount Everest.

96_ Stokes Croft China

'Peculiar china for a peculiar society'

According to its own literature, the People's Republic of Stokes Croft (PRSC) 'embodies an idea and an attitude'. Praised by many but also disliked by those who criticise their methods, the PRSC has been at the forefront of a sometimes losing battle over the gentrification of the area, reclaiming neglected spaces, and often using street art and direct action to highlight issues including land ownership, community empowerment and authority over public space.

PRSC may believe in anti-consumerism, but they finance their activities by selling beautiful and sometimes laugh-out-loud wares. The outside of the Stokes Croft China shop is painted in their signature 'blue rose' pattern, originally created by a Staffordshire pottery whose prints were salvaged by PRSC founder Chris Chalkley. The motif, often combined with the 'Bristol scroll', is now used on mugs, plates, teapots and even a toilet, all for sale here. One shelf is devoted to Tony Benn, the MP for Bristol South East from 1963 to 1983, featuring his quote, 'Hope is the fuel of progress and fear is the prison in which you put yourself'.

Someone else making a regular appearance is *Ursa*, a black-and-white sculpture of a bear, built in the PRSC yard by artist Jamie Gillman, that until 2019 was in the Bearpit (the sunken St James Barton roundabout [see ch. 10]). Even a police riot helmet is on display, with some prints remembering the Stokes Croft riots of 2011, prompted by the opening of a Tesco on nearby Cheltenham Road and the eviction of squatters from a building on the opposite side of the street.

At the back of the shop is also one of the best collections of books about Bristol in the city, with plenty of left-leaning tomes in the spirit of Stokes Croft. Don't miss the postcards either, featuring the winners of the 'Proper Bristol' photography competition and including scenes such as an abandoned sofa and Bristol gig-going legend Jeffrey Johns, known to everybody as Big Jeff.

Address 35 Jamaica Street, BS2 8JP, +44 (0)117 944 4540, sales@prsc.org.uk, www.prscshop.co.uk | Getting there 1-minute walk from Stokes Croft, 5-minute walk from bus station; bus 70, 73, 75 or 76 Stokes Croft or Cheltenham Road | Hours Mon–Sat 11am–6pm, Sun noon–5pm | Tip At the Well on Cheltenham Road is a cafe-cum-launderette founded and run by three sisters. Enjoy an excellent coffee and stack of American pancakes while your clothes are being washed (www.at-the-well.co.uk).

97_Sweetmart

The world's flavours under one roof

Kassam Ismail Majothi fled to England from Uganda in 1972 with his wife and their six children. They ended up in a refugee camp in Somerset with nothing, having left their possessions and money behind in the rush to leave their home country. Fast-forward four decades and Kassam's sons are now in charge of this thriving family business Kassam built up from scratch. Sweetmart has several locations along St Mark's Road in Easton: their main shop with 9,000 products including an unrivalled selection of fresh food (check out the stories under the photos on the walls telling its proud history); a deli cooking authentic Indian food on the premises using recipes passed down through the generations – try the fiery parsnips and samosa chaat; and a wholesale business that counts most of Bristol's Indian restaurants as its customers, and in the 2020 coronavirus pandemic provided food to restaurants such as Chai Shai in Hotwells, which were closed to the public but still cooking meals for NHS staff.

Inside the shop, around half of the products on the packed shelves cannot be found in any supermarket, so both professionals and home cooks rely on them. The family offer several dozen coconut products alone, and more than 100 different chilli sauces. First-timers will leave astounded by the selection on offer and even regulars coming for years will find a new herb, spice or variety of vegetable. Sweetmart's customers have become more discerning over the decades. They no longer ask for Mediterranean spice, seeking instead Moroccan, Syrian, Tunisian or Egyptian. If you're going to find an unusual foodstuff anywhere in Bristol, it'll be here. And if you're interested in more cultural flavour, every year the team help to organise a Grand Iftar on the road outside their shop, with thousands of people eating together and learning more about Ramadan and the Muslim faith.

Address St Mark's Road, Easton, BS5 6JH, +44 (0)117 951 2257, sales@sweetmart.co.uk, www.sweetmart.co.uk | **Getting there** Bus 24 or 49 to Stapleton Road; train to Stapleton Road station | **Hours** Mon–Sat 9am–7pm, Sun 11am–5pm | **Tip** Easton Jamia Mosque is one of the oldest places of worship for Muslims in the South West. A £300,000 refurbishment that finished in 2017 saw it get a beautiful new glass dome (www.eastonjamiamasjid.co.uk).

98 Temple Church
Bristol's own leaning tower of Pisa

Among all of the architects who have plied their trade in Bristol over the centuries, particular credit must be given to the chutzpah of the unknown person who resumed work on the tower of Temple Church. Work started on the tower in the 1390s when the lower three stages were constructed, but was swiftly halted when it began to lean. Yet that did not stop one plucky architect, with building optimistically resumed in roughly 1460 when the top stage was added. It was built with a deliberate correction – the addition of a true vertical on top of the leaning base – but that too is no longer vertical, due to the fact that the tower has continued to tilt, today leaning five feet.

The extraordinary thing is that the tower is not even the most extraordinary thing about Temple Church. The church was originally built here in about 1150 in a highly unusual oval shape by the Knights Templar, a medieval military order founded in the early 12th century to protect pilgrims in the Holy Land. The Templars were 'warrior monks' who obeyed religious vows of chastity and poverty while training for war. The shape of the original church can still be seen marked on the ground, built to recall the Church of the Holy Sepulchre in Jerusalem and the largest of only a dozen such churches in England.

But by 1307, the order had fallen into disrepute and their lands were later confiscated and handed to the Knights Hospitaller. When they were suppressed in turn by King Henry VIII in 1540, the church became a parish church.

The interior was refitted in the 18th century, but the church was bombed during World War II and gutted by fire. Fortunately, some of its original furnishings survive elsewhere, including screens and a sword rest at the Lord Mayor's Chapel (see ch. 67), a 15th-century candelabrum at Bristol Cathedral, and the 18th-century font at Holy Cross church in Knowle.

Address Victoria Street, BS1 6HS | **Getting there** 5-minute walk from Temple Meads, 5-minute walk from St Nick's Market | **Hours** Unrestricted access to exterior | **Tip** The King's Head pub on Victoria Street dates back to the 17th century and has an intact interior c. 1865, including a tramcar-style seating area which is included on CAMRA's National Inventory as being of 'outstanding historic importance'.

99__ That Thing
Fabulous festival fashion

There is a particular emphasis on festival fashion at That Thing, a shop on Stokes Croft named after a song by Lauryn Hill, who coincidentally headlined The Downs festival in Bristol in summer 2019. Stock up on biodegradable glitters, colourful bum bags, furry earrings and after-party tickets. Elsewhere, graffiti spray paint and pens sit on shelves next to mugs and sequined headdresses. On rails hang clothes from dozens of independent designers, including many from Bristol. Up a small flight of stairs is the homeware section, featuring everything from notebooks to tea strainers, vintage mirrors to rugs.

Also upstairs, vintage menswear can be found next to beanie hats, baseball caps, sweatshirts and backpacks branded with the That Thing logo as part of their in-house line, so you can show your love of this shop wherever you go. Anything wrapped in plastic is already on at least its second use, with any plastic packaging unable to be repurposed by the team made into ecobricks: building materials made by stuffing non-recyclable plastic waste inside plastic bottles.

That Thing was founded in 2015 after being forced to change their name from Dutty following an ultimately unsuccessful two-year legal battle with giant Spanish brand Massimo Dutti. Originating as a club night and a platform for women in hip-hop, their ethos is 'to present an up-to-the-minute fresh and eclectic mix of unique pieces, affordable luxury street wear, vintage clothing and lifestyle products'. Vintage at That Thing mostly incorporates fashion from the 1990s, so expect plenty of bright colours and bold prints. In the winter, the work of around 50 independent designers is stocked here, which rises to around 60 in the summer with even more festival wear-orientated brands – perfect for Bristol festivals such as Love Saves the Day.

Address 45-47 Stokes Croft, BS1 3QP, info@thatthing.co, www.thatthing.co | Getting there 4-minute walk from bus station; bus 70, 73, 75 or 76 to Stokes Croft | Hours Mon–Sat 10am–6pm | Tip Pieminister was founded on Stokes Croft, where they still have a restaurant and their head office. Purveyors of mighty fine pies (including vegan option Kevin), they also have restaurants in St Nick's Market and Broad Quay as well as across the UK (www.pieminister.co.uk).

100 Thunder Run

18th-century surround sound

In the days before Dolby Surround Sound, sound effects at the theatre were somewhat more rudimentary. High up in the eaves of Bristol Old Vic, the oldest-surviving theatre in the English-speaking world, one of these late-18th-century methods can still be glimpsed. Spherical iron weights rolled down wooden troughs were once used to replicate the rumbling sound of thunder for the audience below, who would hear the peals reverberating high above their heads. This 'thunder run' is one of only three working examples in the UK and the oldest by 130 years. It is not just a heritage asset either, and was restored during the historic auditorium's 2012 redevelopment and used in the 2016 production of *King Lear* as part of the theatre's 250th anniversary celebrations. The phrase, 'to steal someone's thunder', actually comes from when a rival production stole the thunder-making machine from London's Drury Lane Theatre in 1706.

When the thunder run was once again unveiled after remaining hidden for decades, Bristol Old Vic artistic director Tom Morris said that 'stripping away the theatre's facades has been like a detective story'. Much of that can now be told thanks to a grant from the Heritage Lottery Fund, with a team from the Bristol Old Vic working with the University of Bristol Theatre Collection (see ch. 106) and Bristol Archives to shine a light on some amazing stories from the theatre's past, with plenty of drama both on and offstage. If you are not able to make it to an official heritage tour of the theatre, let the wonders of modern technology take you back in time through your own digital device. Window to the Past allows you to discover what the foyer looked like during the 1770s, 1860s, 1910s and 1970s thanks to a dozen different three-dimensional scenes being mapped onto the current foyer so you can match old spaces with the new configuration as you explore.

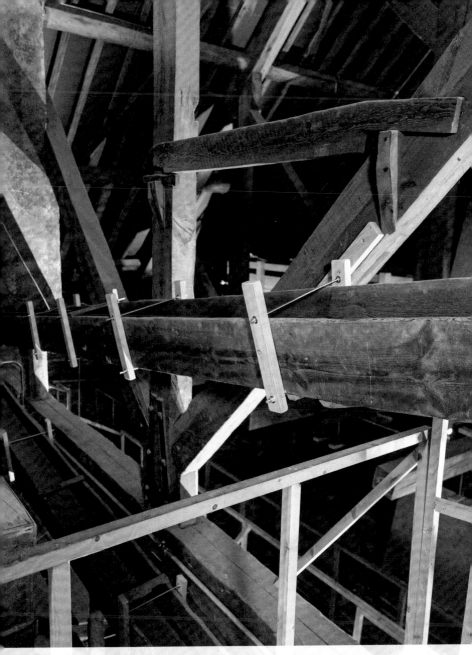

Address Bristol Old Vic, King Street, BS1 4ED, +44 (0)117 987 7877, www.bristololdvic.org.uk/heritage | Getting there 2-minute walk from Queen Square, 3-minute walk from Broad Quay bus stops | Hours Check website for details of what's on | Tip South of the river, the Tobacco Factory Theatres are two theatre spaces within a former tobacco factory on North Street in Bedminster (www.tobaccofactorytheatres.com).

101 Tobacco Factory Market

A symbol of regeneration

The Tobacco Factory Sunday Market started in 2004 and is symbolic of the revitalisation of this corner of south Bristol. As its name suggests, what is now the Tobacco Factory – a bar, restaurant and theatre – used to make cigarettes, with this remnant one of the very few buildings still standing. Based in its car park, the market has a focus on food, but stallholders also sell plants, jewellery, clothes and more. A mixture of delicious smells comes from street-food traders including Gopal's Curry Shack's curry, For Mice & Men's grilled cheese sandwiches and Agnes Spencer's jerk chicken, made by former city poet Miles Chambers. If you're still not feeling warm, grab a drink from Rolling Italy, who serve coffee roasted by Extract in St Werburgh's out of their red Piaggio Ape three-wheeler.

But the first thing that you must do when arriving at the market is to find Farro. This bakery founded by Bradley Tapp started off as a market stall before opening their first permanent premises on Bond Street in 2019. All Sunday mornings are better when fuelled by Farro's canelés and croissants, with a loaf of bread taken to enjoy at home. Like Farro, another market stall which started life here and has since moved into permanent premises is the Bristol Cheesemonger, whose shop can be found within a converted shipping container in Wapping Wharf. And their journey has come full circle, with a second shop now open in the Makers Market. If you can't make it to the Sunday Market, the next best thing is to head to this one. Open six days a week on the ground floor of the Tobacco Factory, stalls include those selling artwork and ceramics, as well as children's activities and a cafe selling produce entirely grown on the Tobacco Factory's own farm in north Somerset. Future plans for the Makers Market include more stalls and practical services such as clothes repair.

Address Raleigh Road, Bedminster, BS3 1TF, www.tobaccofactory.com/markets | **Getting there** Bus 24 to North Street | **Hours** Sun 10am–2.30pm | **Tip** El Rincon on North Street is a typically Spanish tapas bar as well as hosting live music and Spanish language classes for everyone from beginners to experts (www.elrinconbar.com).

102 Tramway Rail Monument
A lasting memory of the Bristol Blitz

Described by Queen Elizabeth I in 1574 as the 'fairest, goodliest and most famous parish church in England', St Mary Redcliffe is currently being brought bang up to date with a brand-new building overlooking Redcliffe Way. Bristol-based architects Purcell, winners of an international design competition, describe their project as representing 'a once-in-a-lifetime opportunity to repair the fault lines that exist in Redcliffe's urban fabric and, in doing so, to position the church at the physical, spiritual and social heart of the city'.

St Mary Redcliffe's origins date back to the 12th century, but within its grounds is a monument to an event in living memory. On 11 April, 1941 – Good Friday and the final day of the 20-week Bristol Blitz – a bomb exploded in a nearby street, throwing a rail from the tramway over the houses. The rail embedded itself in the churchyard close to Colston Parade.

An inscription reads that 'it is left to remind us how narrowly the church escaped destruction in the war 1939–1945'. Legend has it that if you can draw the rail from the ground, you will become the king of Bristol.

It is thought that German pilots used the landmark as an orientation point when navigating above the city, so it is very fortunate to have survived the Blitz with only this rail as damage. Churches like St Mary le Port (see ch. 89) and several others in Bristol didn't have such luck. If it's any consolation to them, St Mary Redcliffe was not so lucky during a 15th-century storm when a bolt of lightning destroyed its original medieval spire. The spire was finally repaired in the 1870s. It only lost its title of the tallest building in Bristol during the construction of Castle Park View tower in 2020, the same year in which a window inside the church dedicated to slave trader Edward Colston was removed a few days after the toppling of his statue in the city centre.

Address Colston Parade, Redcliffe, BS1 6RA, www.stmaryredcliffe.co.uk | Getting there 7-minute walk from Bristol Temple Meads, 5-minute walk from Queen Square | Hours Unrestricted | Tip Inside the church, the 'chaotic pendulum', installed in 1997, runs continuously thanks to a constant flow of recycled water into the centre of a vertical cross beam. Which way will it tip? Even with all the science and maths in the world, it is impossible to predict.

103 __ Trinity
Birthplace of the Bristol Sound

The mission statement of Trinity 'is to empower communities through arts and make sure everyone has the opportunity to access and shape arts and culture in Bristol'. Trinity is a cultural hub for east Bristol, with live music drawing in some big names away from the city centre, as well as an eclectic programme of arts, heritage and cultural activities that Trinity's trustees hope both reach and represent the communities of our diverse city. Regular workshops and classes include Gerry's Attic Dance Company for senior citizens; samba drumming and dancing with Bristol Samba; and stay-and-play sessions for children aged up to five and their carers. Making Tracks is a music-making project offering young people guidance to help develop their creativity through music-making. This could see them performing on Trinity's main stage – with acts playing here including Massive Attack, Public Enemy and Gorillaz – as well as showcase sets at Trinity's annual garden party, St Paul's Carnival and the Harbour Festival.

What is now Trinity was originally the Church of the Holy Trinity, built in 1829 to cope with Bristol's growing population spreading eastwards. It was able to seat at least 2,000 people drawn from an area that was originally known as New Town. The church was closed in the 1970s and was first run by the African-Caribbean Community Enterprise Group and since 2004 has been managed by Trinity Community Arts. One of the church's former memorials is now on display in the foyer of nearby Trinity Road police station. It commemorates PC Richard Hill, who was murdered while off-duty in 1869 in Braggs Lane opposite the church. Hill had intervened when he saw a pair of drunken men abusing a donkey in the street, and died after he was stabbed in the leg. His funeral attracted thousands of mourners, who also lined the route to his burial at Arnos Vale Cemetery (see ch. 5).

Address Trinity Road, Lawrence Hill, BS2 0NW, +44 (0)117 935 1200, info@trinitybristol.org.uk, www.trinitybristol.org.uk | Getting there 5-minute walk from Old Market Street; bus 7 or 24 to Lamb Street | Hours Check website for details of events | Tip The Wardrobe Theatre's first home was above the White Bear pub in Kingsdown. Find it now at the rear of the Old Market Assembly bar and restaurant (www.thewardrobetheatre.com).

104 Troopers Hill

Industrial past, wildlife present

Dominated by its distinctive chimney, the land around Troopers Hill was quarried and mined for hundreds of years. Due to its commanding views across the city, parliamentarian troops camped here prior to the siege of Bristol in 1645 during the English Civil War, and possibly gave the area its name. Its history is much longer than this, however, with the underlying rock formed in the carboniferous period 300 million years ago. Copper smelting was established here in the 18th century, with copper ore brought by boat from Cornwall and Devon, and coal sourced locally. The copper produced was mostly used in the manufacture of brass, with many of these brass products exported to Africa to be bartered for slaves as part of the infamous 'triangular trade'.

The chimney at the top of the hill is 15.92 metres high and originally would have been half this tall again, as previously a brick section stood on top of the existing stone structure. It is thought that the chimney was probably built in the 1790s to serve a new copper works, with Stone & Tinson chemical works continuing to use it until World War I. Bristol City Council is now responsible for its maintenance.

Troopers Hill became a Local Nature Reserve in 1995 in recognition of its wide range of wildlife and its importance as a unique habitat in the Bristol area due to the presence of acidic soils. The hill is an important breeding ground for several rare species of mining bees – the red and black *Andrena integra* and the endangered *Nomada guttulata*, which was discovered on the hill in 2000 and acts like a cuckoo by laying its eggs in other bees' holes. It is home to some bigger animals as well, with the resident foxes and badgers able to enjoy one of the best places in the city to watch the mass ascents of dozens of hot air balloons at the annual Bristol International Balloon Fiesta.

Address BS5 8BL, www.troopers-hill.org.uk | Getting there Bus 44, 45 or 37 to Air Balloon Road | Hours Unrestricted | Tip Crew's Hole Road Footbridge, near the bottom of Troopers Hill, opened in 1957. It replaced the St Anne's ferry, which had been in existence since the Middle Ages.

105 Unicorns

Mythical? They're everywhere!

It is rumoured that the posterior of one of the two unicorns at either end of City Hall was positioned in exactly the right place so that a rival of the building's architect would look straight at the mythical buttocks when he opened his curtains at home every morning. The 12-foot tall, gilt-bronze animals by sculptor David McFall were not part of the building's original plans, with architect E. Vincent Harris ordering them without the council's knowledge. As they were due to be lifted into place, the chairman of the building committee put a stop to their erection as he said he 'knew nothing about the unicorns at all until today'. *The Daily Express* front page of 7 October, 1950 covered the news with the headline, 'Well, who ordered unicorns anyway?' On Harris' return from a holiday in Italy, he explained that the unicorns would be cheaper than the decorative ridging the council had planned.

Bristol's association with unicorns dates back to 1569 when they appeared on the city seal. According to the City Audit Books of the time, unicorns were chosen as they will 'only do homage to men of virtue'. The city's modern coat of arms is based on this ancient seal and features a ship and the keep of Bristol Castle (see ch. 19) between two unicorns. The University of Bristol's original coat of arms used to have a unicorn, but that has been changed on its modern logo to a plain old horse. A unicorn remains across the bow of the SS *Great Britain* and above the pulpit of St John on the Wall church on Broad Street.

Bringing the story of unicorns in Bristol up to date are the city's two 'unicorn' businesses: the privately owned start-up companies valued at more than $1bn. In 2020 there were reported to be only 400 of these companies across the world, with 16 of them based in the UK and two in Bristol: energy provider Ovo Energy and machine intelligence specialists Graphcore.

Address Various locations | Tip Did unicorns hitch a lift on Noah's Ark alongside dinosaurs? That's a question to ask at Noah's Ark Zoo Farm, which has more than 100 species of big animals (www.noahsarkzoofarm.co.uk).

106 UoB Theatre Collection

Centuries-old treasures still inspiring new work

A silk dressing gown and scribbled scripts sit side by side with chocolate wrappers that were dropped down beneath the seats of the stalls at the Bristol Old Vic and rediscovered during the recent renovation of its main auditorium. Just some of the University of Bristol Theatre Collection's other treasures include a 16th-century map of London showing a bear-baiting pit on the site of the future Globe Theatre; an inspirational set design from 1956 made out of cardboard and still held together by masking tape; and the death mask of Sir Henry Irving, one of the most famous of English actors and the first of his profession to be knighted, in 1895, for services to the stage.

More than two million items are stored in the collection's current home in a former printing works, with its 1.5 miles of shelves making it one of the world's largest archives of British theatre history. Its importance was marked in 2020 when the collection was awarded 'designated' status by Arts Council England, which recognises, celebrates and champions collections of national and international significance held outside national museums.

Despite having items in its collection dating back centuries, preserving the past, one of its principal benefits is the inspiration of new work.

The collection may be part of the university, but it is open to everyone and is free to visit, although it does welcome donations. Acclaimed producer Sir Cameron Mackintosh called the collection 'a fine source of creative invention', while author, screenwriter and University of Bristol graduate David Nicholls described it as 'a treasure trove of rare and significant material'. The Theatre Collection is the culmination of more than 60 years of support from actors, collectors, designers, directors, performers and writers all of whom have helped build this remarkable resource.

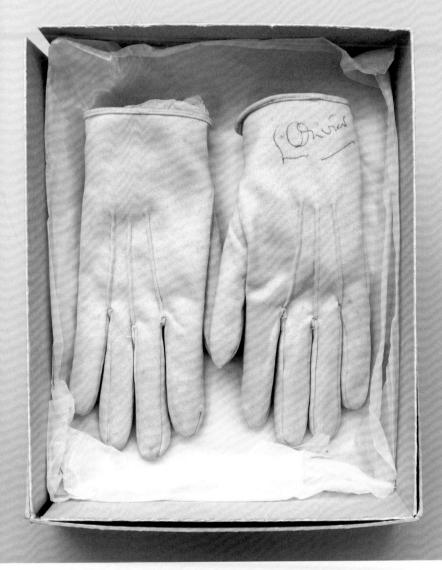

Address Vandyck Building, 21 Park Row, BS1 5LT, +44(0)117 331 5045, theatre-collection@bristol.ac.uk, www.bristol.ac.uk/theatre-collection | Getting there 3-minute walk from Wills Memorial Building; 2-minute walk from top of Christmas Steps | Hours Tue – Fri 9.30am – 5pm | Tip Boarded up for more than two decades due to a dwindling congregation, plans were well afoot in 2020 to transform St Michael on the Mount Without, one of Bristol's oldest churches, into a new dance and theatre event space (www.impermanence.co.uk).

107__Vale Street

The steepest residential road in the UK

If you arrive into Bristol by train at Temple Meads, you might catch a glimpse of the colourful houses on top of a hill in the distance. This is Totterdown, and for many years its residents have claimed that their neighbourhood is the most precipitous in the city. This was officially confirmed in 2019 when the Ordnance Survey named Vale Street as the steepest residential street in the UK. Vale Street's 22-degree average gradient makes it steeper than second-place Old Wyche Road in Great Malvern at 17.54 degrees, followed by roads in Sheffield, Lincoln and Shaftesbury. Its comfortable position at the top of the list is unlikely to be challenged any time soon. It's a street so steep that people living there have been known to tie their cars to lampposts to stop them from rolling away. Cyclists use it as a test of their mettle, and it features on a website dedicated to the world's most dangerous roads.

If you fancy yourself as the polka-dot jersey holder in the Tour de France, given every year to the best climber, get on two wheels to tackle the ride called the 'Bastard Hills of North Bristol'. It takes in some of the maddest, baddest and downright ugliest hills that Montpelier, Kingsdown, Clifton and Cliftonwood have got to offer, such as Brook Hill, Marlborough Hill, Ninetree Hill, Constitution Hill and Bridge Valley Road. These names send shivers down the spines of cyclists, but, although Bridge Valley Road has twice featured as the final climb in the Tour of Britain, they aren't a patch on Vale Street.

On Easter Day, Totterdown residents gather at the top of Vale Street for an annual egg-rolling competition. The decades-old tradition sees hard-boiled eggs bump their way down to the bottom of the road, with the one that gets the furthest declared the winner. There is no prize other than eternal glory and a place in Totterdown's record books.

Address Totterdown, BS4 3BT | Getting there Walk uphill from the number 1 bus stop on Bath Road or downhill from the number 2 stop on Wells Road | Hours Unrestricted | Tip Front Room Arts Trail is a free, annual, weekend-long event in Totterdown, when you can step into the homes of artists to admire and buy their work (www.frontroom.org.uk).

108 Wellington T2905 Memorial

Not your usual balloon ride

On the evening of Wednesday, 30 April, 1941, the six-man crew of a Wellington bomber were on a night exercise from their base in Cambridge towards Sharpness in Gloucestershire. Somehow, they ended up a dozen miles off course flying over Bristol. Due to its importance in World War II, with docks, factories and an airfield, the city had plenty of defences which included barrage balloons placed in strategic locations. The left wing of the T2905 struck the cable of one of these balloons, tethered in Whitehall in the east of the city. The plane flew on, attached to a cable with parachutes at either end, losing height and speed, clipping the cable of another balloon in Easton. Either one cable or the plane's wing hit the chimney of 2 Hurlingham Road in St Andrew's, with a wing also striking a pine tree in St Andrew's Park opposite Norfolk Avenue (the damage can still be seen on the tree today). As the bomber crashed in the park, it split into two and burst into flames. People living nearby ran to help, risking their own lives to pull the airmen out of the plane and taking those injured to their homes, and to the nearest Emergency First Aid Post, which was in the basement of 61 Effingham Road.

Charlie Clarke, Kenneth Evans and Len Lever died in the crash and fire. Hugh Houghton, Stuart Jones and Dickie Wish were rescued. It was while researching his family tree that John Clarke became aware of the full circumstances of the death of his grandfather, Charlie. More research took John to Bristol and to St Andrew's Park, where he was surprised to discover that there was nothing at all to remember the crash. After making contact with the park's friends organisation, John learned that they already had plans to erect a memorial. In 2009, an engraved stone was unveiled in memory of the T2905 crew who died or were injured, and to the bravery of local people.

Address St Andrew's Park, St Andrew's, BS6 5AX | Getting there 5-minute walk from Gloucester Road; 15-minute walk from Montpelier station | Hours Unrestricted | Tip Aerospace Bristol is a museum on the edge of the former Filton Airfield which tells the history of flight, and includes the chance to climb aboard the last Concorde to fly (www.aerospacebristol.org).

109 __ Westbury College

A castle in miniature

Westbury-on-Trym may lie within the boundaries of Bristol but it still has the feel of a self-contained village – which it was until 1904. Westbury is in fact older than Bristol, with flints found in an archaeological dig in the 1960s dating back to the Mesolithic era, indicating that people have lived in the area for at least 7,000 years. A Christian settlement on the banks of the River Trym since the 8th century later became a monastic community and then a collegiate church under a group of canons. These canons evidently had big ambitions, with their residence at Westbury College being completed in 1469 like a miniature castle and planned on the quadrangular system popular at the time in Oxford. The still-imposing structure had towers, turrets and battlements and was deemed so strategically important that it was part-destroyed by Royalists in 1643 during the English Civil War, to prevent it being occupied by Parliamentary forces.

The gatehouse, two corner turrets and part of its wall still survive, with the college's grounds now housing a retirement home, and the gatehouse used by an RAF air cadet squadron and as parish council meeting rooms.

The gatehouse tower was once even higher than it is today due to the street level in medieval times being lower. Look up at it from the outside to see gargoyles beneath the battlements and take a walk around the corner to Trym Road for the best view of the other remaining corner turret. This side of the former Westbury College was perpendicular to the path of the Trym, with excavations on the frontage revealing origins dating back more than 1,000 years. Gatehouse owners, the National Trust, retain ancient permission, known as riparian rights, to this section of the river. So if you fancy doing a bit of fishing here, make sure to bring along your National Trust membership card.

Address College Road, Westbury-on-Trym, BS9 3EH | Getting there 4-minute walk from High Street; served by bus 1 | Hours Unrestricted | Tip 38 Church Road in Westbury-on-Trym, a house dedicated to contemplative prayer, is one of the oldest lived-in buildings in Bristol. Dr Elsie Briggs of the University of Bristol uncovered many of its 15th-century features when she lived here from 1958 to 1988 (www.elsiebriggshouse.org.uk).

110 The Wicker Nose

An enormous olfactory edifice

A sculpture in the leafy suburb of Redland is almost unique in Bristol for being public art on the side of a house that has not been spray-painted. Gable ends of homes across the city are regularly given over to graffiti artists for commissions. But this one is slightly different, because this one is three-dimensional. Not having an official title, the artwork – on the back wall of a house on Roslyn Road but only visible from Kensington Road – is known by a variety of names, including 'the house that smells'.

Like the best stories of old, the origins of the 3.7-metre-high nose are lost in time, giving it a whiff of mystery. Some say it used to be made of papier-mâché, some say concrete, some say it was once even made out of gold. (Although this latter recollection might have been caused by one too many ciders in the nearby Kensington Arms pub.)

This neighbourhood is a popular one with undergraduates, with occasional ill-feeling between permanent residents and noisy students, and the roads noticeably quieter during university holidays. Urban legend has it that members of a rowdy rowing club out late at night broke the original fibreglass nose – here since the mid-1990s – by inserting an oar up one nostril.

'It's in urgent need of a nose job, it's falling apart,' Jane Tarr, who lived in the house, told BBC Bristol after the vandalism in 2007. Schnozzle supporters raised hundreds of pounds to replace the splintered protuberance with community fundraising events. Some of this money is also said to have come from a commuter on the nearby Severn Beach Line (see ch. 94) who enjoyed seeing the artistic anatomy on his way to work. The new nose was created by artist Oliver Hales in his favoured medium of willow, and the sustainable sculpture continues to be a comforting sight for passengers in passing trains between Redland and Clifton Down stations.

Address Roslyn Road, Redland, BS6 6NJ | Getting there 5-minute walk from White-ladies Road; 5-minute walk from Redland railway station | Hours Unrestricted | Tip The Kensington Arms (the Kenny to its regulars) is one of Bristol's best gastropubs. Since 2016 it has been co-owned by Josh Eggleton of the Michelin-starred Pony & Trap in Chew Magna (www.thekensingtonarms.co.uk).

111 Zion

Deconsecrated, but far from dead

Zion is one of those places in Bristol that are impossible to define in just one sentence, and which are many different things to many different people. Its varied programme of events throughout the typical week encompasses everything from music to theatre, craft to circus. Artwork from local residents is displayed on the walls and a cafe is a popular social hub for young and old. Community focus is the key here for Jess Wright, who saw the potential in a derelict building. Zion is now run as a not-for-profit social enterprise, with all its income used to help create a sustainable future for the building and the eclectic events that take place within it. These also include weddings, which is fitting. It used to be a Methodist chapel, which held its last service in 2008 due to a dwindling congregation.

Zion is just one of many former churches in Bristol that have been given new leases of life. These include St Paul's Church in Portland Square in St Paul's, now used for circus training by Circomedia (see ch. 37); St Werburgh's Church on Mina Road in St Werburgh's (moved here almost brick by brick from Corn Street in 1877 due to road widening, and which gave the area then known as Baptist Mills its new name) is now a climbing centre; and Bristol's former Catholic cathedral on Park Place in Clifton was home to a school and a temporary arts venue before being transformed into luxury student flats.

During the coronavirus pandemic of 2020, the Zion community came together for a project to mark their time during lockdown. Each participant was given a date and it was up to them to document their day, through writing, drawing, photography, poetry or music. The entries were then posted on a Facebook page for the whole community to see, with the aim to publish two books, one for adults and another for children to remember the community's resilience and creativity.

Address Bishopsworth Road, Bedminster Down, BS13 7JW, +44 (0)117 923 1212, info@zionbristol.co.uk, www.zionbristol.co.uk | Getting there Bus 75 to Bishopsworth Road; 10-minute walk from Parson Street railway station | Hours Tue – Sat 9am – 4.30pm | Tip Just a 5-minute walk away, Manor Woods Valley is a nature reserve with wildflower meadows, woodland and plenty of wildlife, running alongside the Malago stream (www.manorwoodsvalley.org).

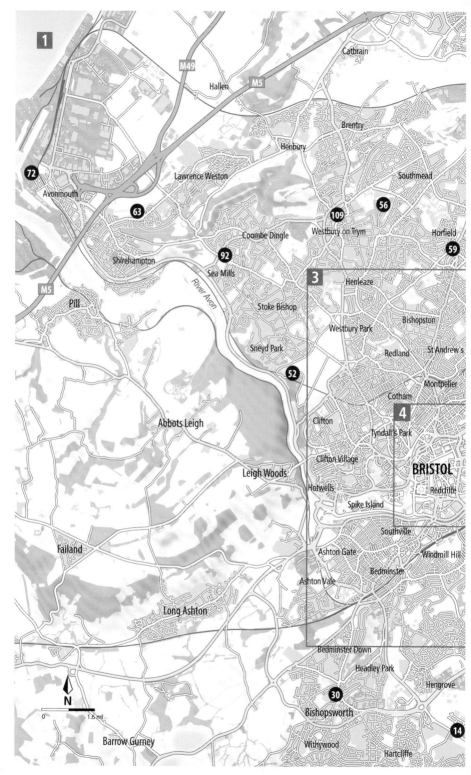

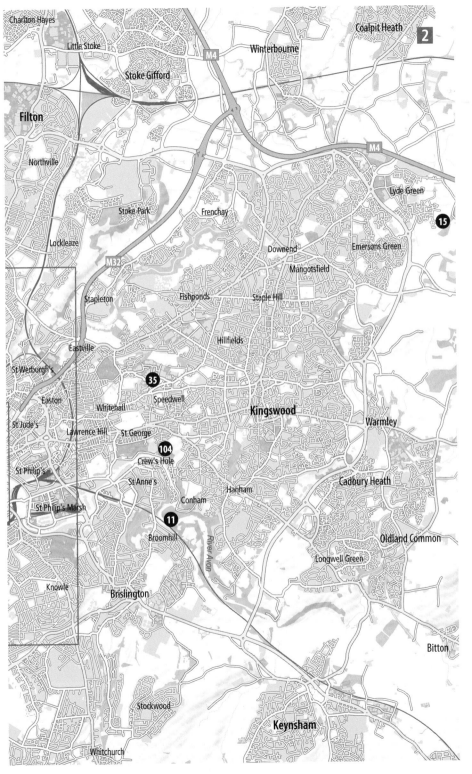

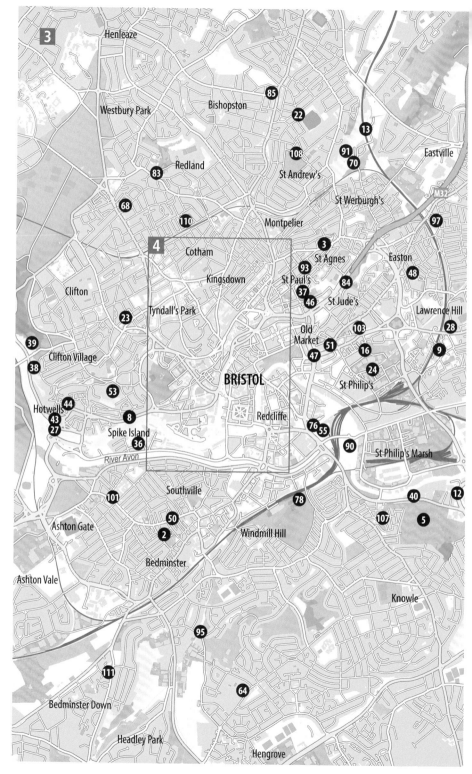

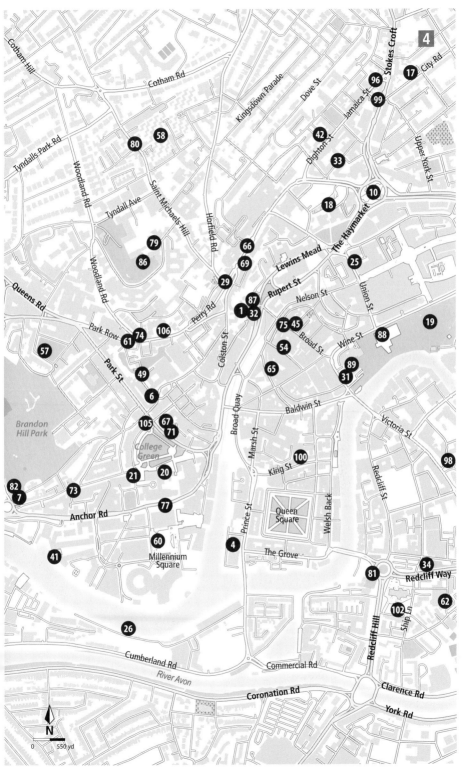

Bibliography

The Archaeology of the County of Somerset, D. P. Dobson (Methuen, 1931)

Archaeology National Trust SW (archaeologynationaltrustsw.wordpress.com)

Bravo, Bristol! The City at War 1914-1918, Eugene Byrne (Redcliffe Press, 2014)

Bristol, Andrew Foyle (Pevsner Architectural Guides, 2009)

Bristol Archive Records: www.bristolarchiverecords.com

Bristol Boys Make More Noise!, Gill Loats (Tangent Books, 2014)

The Bristol High Cross, M. J. H. Liversidge (Bristol Branch of the Historical Association, 1978)

Central Bristol Through the Ages, Anthony Beeson (Amberley Publishing, 2017)

The Curious History of Mazes: 4,000 Years of Fascinating Twists and Turns, Julie E. Bounford (Wellfleet Press, 2018)

The Dispensaries: Healthcare for the Poor Before the NHS, Michael Whitfield (AuthorHouse, 2016)

The English Spa, 1560-1815: A Social History, Phyllis May Hembry (Fairleigh Dickinson Univ Press, 1990)

The History of the Bristol Region in the Roman Period, David Higgins (Bristol Branch of the Historical Association, 2005)

Hotwells: Spa to Pantomime, Sue Stops (Bristol Books, 2020)

House-names of Shirehampton and Avonmouth, Richard Coates (Shire Community Newspaper, 2013)

The Industrial Archaeology of Bristol, R. A. Buchanan (Bristol Branch of the Historical Association, 1967)

The Industrial Archaeology of the Bristol & Bath Region (Bristol Industrial Archaeological Society, 2017)

Introducing Bristol Glass, Cleo Witt (Redcliffe Press, 1984)

Kingsdown: Bristol's Vertical Suburb, Penny Mellor (Phillimore & Co, 2009)

Massive Attack: Out of the Comfort Zone, Melissa Chemam (Tangent Books, 2019)

St Bartholomew's Hospital, Bristol: The Excavation of a Medieval Hospital 1976–88, Roger Price with Michael Ponsford (Council for British Archaeology, 1998)

South Bristol Through Time, Will Musgrave (Amberley, 2013)

The Street Names of Bristol, Veronica Smith (Broadcast Books, 2001)

Temple Church, Bristol (Wessex Archaeology, Salisbury, 2000)

Thomas Goldney's Garden, P. K. Stembridge (Burleigh Press, 1996)

Unbuilt Bristol: The City that Might Have Been 1750-2050, Eugene Byrne (Redcliffe Press, 2013)

The University of Bristol Historic Gardens, Marion Mako (University of Bristol, 2011)

Wellington T2905 (www.wellingtont2905.co.uk)

Acknowledgements

To the Bristol Booths: Jo, Mersina and Lois – thank you for your love, support and patience. Jo: thank you for believing in me when I didn't, and supporting me through thick and thin from start to finish. My mum Shelagh and dad Tony, for encouraging me to be a writer from an early age. My aunty Anne for her writing tips. And my grandad, Jim, who was so thrilled when I told him that I was writing this guide and who I wish could have seen it.

Everyone who has helped and armed me with facts along the way. Jon Chamberlain and Shonette Laffy at Visit Bristol, Natalie Fee, Pete Insole from Know Your Place, Philippa Walker and Richard Cottle at the University of Bristol, Jo Elsworth at the University of Bristol Theatre Collection, Rob Acton-Campbell at Friends of Troopers Hill, Mark Taylor, Ani Stafford Townsend, David Martyn, Network Rail, Historic England, Gill Loats, Chris Kelly, Martin Papworth, Westbury-on-Trym Society, Nick Howes, Amanda Adams and Tom Morris at Bristol Old Vic, Paul Blakemore, Jon Craig, Daniel Durrans, Nick Howes, Holly Jones and Clare Gosling at acta, and Caitlin Clark at Bristol City Council.

Kate Dawson for all of her optimism and advice. Tash Ebbs for telling me to keep on writing. And an extra special thanks to Reeve Hicks for keeping an eye on my bag with the laptop in containing the only copy of this book, which I accidentally left in the Lion playpark in Cliftonwood after visiting with my daughters.

My brilliant editor, Alison Lester, who ensured that the words in this book were all shipshape and Bristol fashion. I could not have chosen a better person to have discussions about commas, semi-colons and italics. Cheers, drive! Everyone at Emons. Thank you for turning this idea into a reality even as the world turned upside down. And of course, Bristol's most brilliant photographer, Barbara Evripidou, aka Babs. Thank you for making our book look even more awesome than we could have imagined.

To the people who I had conversations with while in the midst of writing in various locations across Bristol – and then over Twitter while finishing the last dozen or so at home during the coronavirus lockdown: Adam Tutton, Amy Grace, Anna Rutherford, Anna Starkey, Aphra Evans, Beryl Dzambo, Caitlin Bowring, Chris Chubb, Claire Stewart, Clare Reddington, Dave Cullen, Dave Moss, Dick Penny, Frankie Wallington, George Ferguson, Gus Hoyt, Izzy Biggin, Jen Forster, Josh Eggleton, Kamalpreet Badasha, Kelly Sidgwick, Liz Harkman, Lizzie Murray, Lucy Holloway, Mark Chapman, Mark Cosgrove, Nigel Muntz, Paul Parry, Ri Meredith, Rich Grundy, Rich Warren, Richard Tring, Roger Griffiths, Sarah Robertson, Stephen Lightbown, Tom Tainton and many others.

Alex and Kate Steel, Jess Brown, and everybody at F45 Bristol Central, who kept my body moving after hours crouched at a laptop. Everybody at Bristol24/7, especially my full-time editorial team of Ellie Pipe and Lowie Trevena for keeping the ship afloat while I took time off to write this book.

The staff of Boston Tea Party, the Arnolfini, Bristol Central Library, Cloakroom Cafe, Convoy Espresso, Crofter Coffee, Daily Grind, Downtown Taqueria, East Village Cafe, Emmeline, Folk House Cafe, Foliage, Friska, Glitch, Little Victories, Mark's Bread, Mokoko, Pickle at Underfall Yard, the Severn Beach Line, St Werburgh's City Farm Cafe and Society Cafe; and especially at Full Court Press, Small Street Espresso and the Watershed – where most of this book was written fuelled by cortados, cold brews and craft beer.

Martin Booth

Huge thanks to Martin & Joanna Booth for their continual support throughout the process and their faith in my work and thank you to our publishers Emons: for being so lovely to work with.

A massive thank you to everyone at all the places we've included who helped me with getting the photos, particularly during these difficult times, and the easier times. A credit to you all for being so accommodating with my requests. A special mention to Guildhall Chambers for allowing me to shoot the Everard's Printing Works from their offices, Julia and Oliver at the Ken Stradling Collection for replying to my constant queries, Alison at The Cube and Katie & Clare at acta for going beyond the call of duty in getting the best shot, Taj at The Passenger Shed, Dave at The Bristol Old Vic, Lindsay at Broadmead Baptist Church, Steph at The Orchard, the teams at The Exchange, Stokes Croft China, That Thing, UoB Theatre Collection, Felix Road Playground, The Folk House and Glitch, Sarah at Room 212, Ani at The Milliners Guild, Nick at the Letterpress Collective, Alison at Henleaze Lake, Norman at Sweetmart, Luke at The Bag of Nails and Tim & Andre at Campus Pool Skatepark for giving me my first 'real' coffee three months into lockdown.

To my dear friends who have supported me emotionally, especially Jackie, Emily, Lucy, Rachel, Vicki, Jenny, Sangee, Becky, Jane, Toni, Freia, Chrissie, Sam, Joolie, Mary, the SR crew, Tandy and Michael Lloyd for my lovely portrait - you know I've always been happier behind the camera rather than in front of it.

Finally thank you to my wonderful kids, Theo and Anna, for being so patient with me, to my partner Paul who kept me focused and in bottomless cups of tea, and to my ever-supportive, amazing and growing family, Mum and Dad, Anna, Pete, Carina, Leo and Amelia, but especially my Mum and Dad. Dad, I'm sorry you're not here to see the book, but I know how proud you were that I was going on this journey.

Barbara Evripidou

Martin Booth is the editor of Bristol24/7, the city's leading news and entertainment website, and free monthly magazine. Martin has previously written for publications including *The Times*, *The Guardian*, *Time Out* and the 2007 FA Cup semi-final programme. In his spare time, he enjoys cycling, travelling and drinking locally-brewed beer. He lives in Bristol with his wife, Jo, and their two daughters, Mersina and Lois. Follow him on Twitter for all things Bristol and more at @beardedjourno.

Barbara Evripidou is an award-winning photographer with three decades of experience. As a former press photographer, her images have been published in all the UK's national newspapers, and she has worked all over the world. The highlight of her career was working with the British Army in Bosnia, covering the efforts to rebuild the country. These days she focuses on PR, portrait and commercial work. When she's not got a camera in her hand you can find her at a metal gig, at the cinema or exploring Bristol – where she lives with her children, Theo and Anna. Find out more at firstavenuephotography.com.